AQUARIUS
WITCH

©JAMES C. WELCH

Ivo Dominguez, Jr. (Georgetown, DE) has been active in the magickal community since 1978. He is one of the founders of Keepers of the Holly Chalice, the first Assembly of the Sacred Wheel coven. He currently serves as one of the Elders in the Assembly. Ivo is the author of several books, including *The Four Elements of the Wise* and *Practical Astrology for Witches and Pagans*. In his mundane life, he has been a computer programmer, the executive director of an AIDS/HIV service organization, a bookstore owner, and many other things. Visit him at www.ivodominguezjr.com.

© TRISTAN FOX MUELLER

Mickie Mueller (she/her) is a witch, bestselling author, award-winning illustrator, tarot creator, and YouTube content creator. She's written and illustrated multiple books, articles, and tarot decks for Llewellyn Worldwide, including *Mystical Cats Tarot*, *Magical Dogs Tarot*, *The Witch's Mirror*, and *Llewellyn's Little Book of Halloween*. Her magickal art is distributed internationally and has been seen as set dressing on SyFy's *The Magicians* and Bravo's *Girlfriends Guide to Divorce*. Her YouTube videos are shot in her studio where she creates art, writes about witchcraft and folklore, and manifests her own style of eclectic everyday magick. She loves to teach practical and innovative ways to work magick using items and ingredients in your home. Visit her at mickiemueller.com

• UNLOCK THE MAGIC OF YOUR SUN SIGN •

AQUARIUS
WITCH

≈

IVO DOMINGUEZ, JR.
MICKIE MUELLER

Llewellyn Publications
Woodbury, Minnesota

FIRST EDITION
First Printing, 2024

Art direction and cover design by Shira Atakpu
Book design by Christine Ha
Interior art by the Llewellyn Art Department
Illustrations (Aquarius constellation, page 7; floral ornaments, pages 33, 43, 57, 89, & 189; moon, pages 79 & 168; spiked heart, pages 80 & 173; water pitcher, pages 5, 64, & 188; windchimes, page 167 & 221) by Mickie Mueller
Tarot Original 1909 Deck © 2021 with art created by Pamela Colman Smith and Arthur Edward Waite. Used with permission of Lo Scarabeo.
The Aquarius Correspondences appendix is excerpted with permission from *Llewellyn's Complete Book of Correspondences: A Comprehensive & Cross-Referenced Resource for Pagans & Wiccans* © 2013 by Sandra Kynes.

Llewellyn Publications is a registered trademark of Llewellyn Worldwide Ltd.

Library of Congress Cataloging-in-Publication Data
Names: Domínguez, Ivo, Jr., author. | Mueller, Mickie, author.
Title: Aquarius witch : unlock the magic of your sun sign / Ivo Dominguez, Jr., Mickie Mueller.
Description: Woodbury : Llewellyn Worldwide Ltd, 2024. | Series: The witch's sun sign series; 11 | Includes bibliographical references.
Identifiers: LCCN 2024013896 (print) | LCCN 2024013897 (ebook) | ISBN 9780738772905 (paperback) | ISBN 9780738773032 (ebook)
Subjects: LCSH: Aquarius (Astrology) | Witchcraft. | Magic.
Classification: LCC BF1727.7 D66 2024 (print) | LCC BF1727.7 (ebook) | DDC 133.5/276—dc23/eng/20240423
LC record available at https://lccn.loc.gov/2024013896
LC ebook record available at https://lccn.loc.gov/2024013897

Llewellyn Publications
A Division of Llewellyn Worldwide Ltd.
2143 Wooddale Drive
Woodbury, MN 55125-2989
www.llewellyn.com

Printed in the United States of America

Other Books by Ivo Dominguez, Jr.

The Four Elements of the Wise
Keys to Perception: A Practical Guide to Psychic Development
Practical Astrology for Witches and Pagans
Casting Sacred Space
Spirit Speak

Other Books by Mickie Mueller

The Witch's Mirror
Mystical Cats Tarot
Magical Dogs Tarot
Llewellyn's Little Book of Halloween

Other Books in The Witch's Sun Sign Series

Aries Witch
Taurus Witch
Gemini Witch
Cancer Witch
Leo Witch
Virgo Witch
Libra Witch
Scorpio Witch
Sagittarius Witch
Capricorn Witch
Pisces Witch

CONTENTS

Spells, Recipes, and Practices ✳ **xv**

Introduction ✳ **1**

How Your Sun Powers Your Magick (Dominguez) ✳ **9**

Aquarius Correspondences (Dominguez) ✳ **28**

Witchcraft That Comes Naturally to an Aquarius
(Mueller) ✳ **31**

Magical Correspondences (Mueller) ✳ **46**

Timing, Places, and Things (Dominguez) ✳ **49**

Herbal Correspondences (Dominguez) ✳ **68**

Cleansing and Shielding (Mueller) ✳ **71**

What Sets an Aquarius Off, and
How to Recover (Mueller) ✳ **81**

*Pamela "Pixie" Colman Smith:
An Iconic but Almost-Forgotten Aquarian Artist
(Nic Bhé Chuille)* ✳ **93**

The Sway of Your Moon Sign (Dominguez) ✳ **97**

Tarot Correspondences (Dominguez) ✳ **126**

My Most Aquarius Witch Moment (Mueller) ✳ **129**

✳ Contents ✳

Your Rising Sign's Influence (Dominguez) ✳ 137

A Dish Fit for an Aquarius:
Visionary Violet Potato Soup (Hunt) ✳ 161

Recharging and Self-Care (Mueller) ✳ 165

Don't Blame It on Your Sun Sign (Mueller) ✳ 177

Postcard from an Aquarius Witch (Kieran) ✳ 193

Spirit of Aquarius Guidance Ritual (Dominguez) ✳ 197

Aquarius Anointing Oil Recipe (Dominguez) ✳ 213

Better Every Day: The Way Forward (Mueller) ✳ 215

Conclusion (Dominguez) ✳ 223

Appendix: Aquarius Correspondences from Llewellyn's
Complete Book of Correspondences *(Kynes)* ✳ 225

Resources ✳ 229

Contributors ✳ 231

SPELLS, RECIPES, AND PRACTICES

Aquarian Witch Spell to Focus on a Task
by Mickie Mueller ... 38

The Star Card Ritual: Seeking Your Divine Spark
by Danielle Dionne ... 43

A Charging Practice by Ivo Dominguez, Jr ... 65

House Cleansing Practice by Mickie Mueller ... 75

*Summoning Serenity: Crafting Incense and
Conjuring Cool Spirits* by Silver Daniels ... 89

Visionary Violet Potato Soup
by Dawn Aurora Hunt ... 161

A Self-Care Practice to Soothe the Aquarian Mind
by Robin Fennelly ... 174

Become Friends with Time Spell by Mickie Mueller ... 178

Connect with Others Spell Jar by Mickie Mueller ... 182

Aquarius Witch: Altar for the Rebel Mystic
by Sandra Santiago ... 189

Ritual to Meet the Spirit of Your Sign
by Ivo Dominguez, Jr ... 203

Aquarius Anointing Oil Recipe
by Ivo Dominguez, Jr ... 213

INTRODUCTION

Ivo Dominguez, Jr.

This is the eleventh book in the Witch's Sun Sign series. There are twelve volumes in this series with a book for every Sun sign, but with a special focus on witchcraft. This series explores and honors the gifts, perspectives, and joys of being a witch through the perspective of their Sun sign. Each book has information on how your sign affects your magick and life experiences with insights provided by witches of your Sun sign, as well as spells, rituals, and practices to enrich your witchcraft. This series is geared toward helping witches grow, develop, and integrate the power of their Sun sign into all their practices. Each book in the series has ten writers, so there are many takes on the meaning of being a witch of a particular sign. All the books in the Witch's Sun Sign series are a sampler of possibilities, with pieces that are deep, fun, practical, healing, instructive, revealing, and authentic.

Welcome to the Aquarius Witch

I'm Ivo Dominguez, Jr., and I've been a witch and an astrologer for over forty years. In this book, and in the whole series, I've written the chapters focused on astrological information and collaborated with the other writers. For the sake of transparency, I am a Sagittarius, and most of the other writers for this book are Aquarius.[1] The chapters focused on the lived experience of being an Aquarius witch were written by my coauthor, Mickie Mueller. She is an author, an artist, a tarot and oracle deck illustrator, a lover of plant magick, an ordained priestess, and a Reiki master. The spells and shorter pieces written for this book come from a diverse group of strong Aquarius witches. Their practices will give you a deeper understanding of yourself as an Aquarius and as a witch. With the information, insights, and methods offered here, your Aquarius nature and your witchcraft will be better united. The work of becoming fully yourself entails finding, refining, and merging all the parts that make up your life and identity. This all sounds very serious, but the content of this book will run from lighthearted to profound to do justice to the topic. Moreover, this book has practical suggestions on using the power of your Sun sign to improve your craft as a witch. There are many books on

---

1. The exceptions are Dawn Aurora Hunt, who contributes a recipe for each sign in the series, and Sandra Kynes, whose correspondences are listed in the appendix. They are Scorpios.

Aquarius or astrology or witchcraft; this book is about whole-heartedly being an Aquarius witch.

There is a vast amount of material available in books, blogs, memes, and videos targeted at Aquarius. The content presented in these ranges from serious to snarky, and a fair amount of it is less than accurate or useful. After reading this book, you will be better equipped to tell which of these you can take to heart and use, and which are fine for a laugh but not much more. There is a good chance you will be flipping back to reread some chapters to get a better understanding of some of the points being made. This book is meant to be read more than once, and some parts of it may become reference material you will use for years. Consider keeping a folder, digital or paper, for your notes and ideas on being an Aquarius witch.

What You Will Need

Knowing your Sun sign is enough to get quite a bit out of this book. However, to use all the material in this book, you will need your birth chart to verify your Moon sign and rising sign. In addition to your birth date, you will need the location and the time of your birth as exactly as possible. If you don't know your birth time, try to get a copy of your birth certificate (though not all birth certificates list times). If it is reasonable and you feel comfortable, you can ask family members for information. They may remember an exact time, but even narrowing it down to a range of hours will be useful.

There is a solution to not having your exact birth time. Since it takes moments to create birth charts using software, you can run birth charts that are thirty minutes apart over the span of hours that contains your possible birth times. By reading the chapters that describe the characteristics of Moon signs and rising signs, you can reduce the pile of possible charts to a few contenders. Read the descriptions and find the chart whose combination of Moon sign and rising sign rings true to you. There are more refined techniques a professional astrologer can use to get closer to a chart that is more accurate. However, knowing your Sun sign, Moon sign, and rising sign is all you need for this book. There are numerous websites that offer free basic birth charts you can view online. For a fee, more detailed charts are available on these sites.

You may want to have an astrological wall calendar or an astrological day planner to keep track of the sign and phase of the Moon. You will want to keep track of what your ruling planet, Uranus, is doing. Over time as your knowledge grows, you'll probably start looking at where all the planets are, what aspects they are making, and when they are retrograde or direct. You could do this all on an app or a website, but it is often easier to flip through a calendar or planner to see what is going on. Flipping forward and back through the weeks and months ahead can give you a better sense of how to prepare for upcoming celestial influences. Moreover, the calendars and planner contain basic background information about astrology and are a great start for studying astrology.

You're an Aquarius and So Much More

Every person is unique, complex, and a mixture of traits that can clash, complement, compete, or collaborate with each other. This book focuses on your Aquarius Sun sign and provides starting points for understanding your Moon sign and rising sign. It cannot answer all your questions or be a perfect fit because of all the other parts that make you an individual. However, you will find more than enough to enrich and deepen your witchcraft as an Aquarius. There will also be descriptions you won't agree with or you think do not portray you. In some instances, you will be correct, and in other cases, you may come around to acknowledging that the information does apply to you. Astrology can be used for magick, divination, personal development, and more. No matter the purpose, your understanding of astrology

will change over time as your life unfolds and your experience and self-knowledge broaden. You will probably return to this book several times as you find opportunities to use more of the insights and methods.

This may seem like strange advice to find in a book for the Aquarius witch, but remember that you are more than an Aquarius witch. In the process of claiming the identity of being a witch, it is common to want to have a clear and firm definition of who you are. Sometimes this means overidentifying with a category, such as fire witch, herb witch, crystal witch, kitchen witch, and so on. It is useful to become aware of the affinities you have so long as you do not limit and bind yourself to being less than you are. The best use for this book is to uncover all the Aquarius parts of you so you can integrate them well. The finest witches I know have well-developed specialties but also are well rounded in their knowledge and practices.

Onward!

With all that said, the Sun is the starting point for your power and your journey as a witch. The first chapter is about the profound influence your Sun sign has, so don't skip through the table of contents; please start at the beginning. After that, Mickie will dive into magick and practices that come naturally to Aquarius witches. I'll be walking you through the benefits of picking the right times, places, and things to energize your

Aquarius magick. Mickie will also share a couple of real-life personal stories on how to manage the busy lives that Aquarius choose, as well as advice on the best ways to protect yourself spiritually and set good boundaries when you really need to. I'll introduce you to how your Moon sign and your rising sign shape your witchcraft. Mickie offers great stories about how her Aquarius nature comes forward in her life as a witch, and then gives suggestions on self-care and self-awareness. I'll share a full ritual with you to call on the spirit of your sign. Lastly, Mickie offers her wisdom on how to become a better Aquarius witch. Throughout the whole book, you'll find tables of correspondences, spells, recipes, practices, and other treasures to add to your practices.

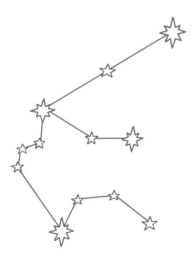

HOW YOUR SUN POWERS YOUR MAGICK

Ivo Dominguez, Jr.

The first bit of astrology people generally learn is their Sun sign. Some enthusiastically embrace the meaning of their Sun sign and apply it to everything in their life. They feel their Sun is shining and all is well in the world. Then at some point, they'll encounter someone who will, with a bit of disdain, enlighten them on the limits of Sun sign astrology. They feel their Sun isn't enough, and they scramble to catch up. What comes next is usually the discovery that they have a Moon sign, a rising sign, and all the rest of the planets in an assortment of signs. Making sense of all this additional information is daunting as it requires quite a bit of learning and/or an astrologer to guide you through the process. Wherever you are on this journey into the world of astrology, at some point you will circle back around and rediscover that the Sun is still in the center.

The Sun in your birth chart shows where life and spirit came into the world to form you. It is the keeper of your spark of spirit and the wellspring of your power. Your Sun is in Aquarius, so that is the flavor, the color, the type of energy that is at your core. You are your whole birth chart, but it is your Aquarius Sun that provides the vital force that moves throughout all parts of your life. When you work in harmony and alignment with your Sun, you have access to more life and the capacity to live it better. This is true for all people, but this advice takes on a special meaning for those who are witches. The root of a witch's magick power is revealed by their Sun sign. You can draw on many kinds of energy, but the type of energy you attract with greatest ease is Aquarius. The more awareness and intention you apply to connecting with and acting as a conduit for that Aquarius Sun, the more effective you will be as a witch.

The more you learn about the meaning of an Aquarius Sun, the easier it will be to find ways to make that connection. To be effective in magick, divination, and other categories of workings, it is vital to understand yourself—your motivations, drives, attractions, etc.—so you can refine your intentions, questions, and desired outcomes. Understanding your Sun sign is an important step in that process. One of the goals shared by both witchcraft and astrology is to affirm and to integrate the totality of your nature to live your best life. The glyph for the Sun in astrology is a dot with a circle around it. Your Aquarius Sun is the dot and the circle, your center, and your circumference. It is your beginning and your journey. It is also the core of your personal Wheel of the Year, the seasons of your life that repeat, have resonances, but are never the same.

How Aquarius Are You?

The Sun is the hub around which the planets circle. Its gravity pulls the planets to keep them in their courses and bends space-time to create the place we call our solar system. The Sun in your birth chart tugs on every other part of your chart in a similar way. Everything is both bound and free, affected but seeking its own direction. When people encounter descriptions of Aquarius traits, they will often begin to make a list of which things apply to them and which don't. Some will say they are the epitome of Aquarius traits, others will claim that they are barely Aquarius, and many will be somewhere in between. Evaluating how closely or not you align with the traditional characteristics of an Aquarius is not a particularly useful approach to understanding your sign. If you are an Aquarius, you have all the Aquarius traits somewhere within you. What varies from person to person is the expression of those traits. Some traits express fully in a classic form, others are blocked from expressing or are modified, and sometimes there is a reaction to behave as the opposite of what is expected. As an Aquarius, and especially as a witch, you have the capacity to activate dormant traits, to shape functioning traits, and to tone down overactive traits.

The characteristics and traits of signs are tendencies, drives, and affinities. Gravity encourages a ball to roll down a hill. A plant's leaves will grow in the direction of sunlight. The warmth of a fire will draw people together on a cold night. A flavor you enjoy will entice you to take another bite of your food. Your Aquarius Sun urges you to be and to act like an Aquarius. That said, you also have free will and volition to make other choices. Moreover, the rest of your birth chart and the ever-changing celestial influences are also shaping your options, moods, and drives. The more you become aware of the traits and behaviors that come with being an Aquarius, the easier it will be to choose how you express them. Most people want to have the power to make their own choices, but for an Aquarius, it is essential.

As a witch, you have additional tools to work with the Aquarius energy. You can choose when to access and how you shape the qualities of Aquarius as they come forth in your life. You can summon the energy of Aquarius, name the traits you desire, and manifest them. You can also banish or

12

neutralize or ground what you don't need. You can find where your Aquarius energy short-circuits, where it glitches, and unblock it. You can examine your uncomfortable feelings and your less-than-perfect behaviors to seek the shadowed places within so you can heal or integrate them. Aquarius is also a spirit and a current of collective consciousness that is vast in size— a group mind and archetype. Aquarius is not limited to humanity; it engages with plants, animals, minerals, and all the physical and nonphysical beings of the Earth and all its associated realms. As a witch, you can call upon and work with the spiritual entity that is Aquarius. You can live your life as a ritual. The motion of your life can be a dance to the tune and rhythm of the heavens.

The Aquarius Glyph

Aquarius's glyph is two parallel zigzags that bring to mind lightning flashes, a channel that guides wind, water, ideas, and images. The glyph's two lines may be completely angular or have a bit of a wavy appearance. In magick, I prefer the sharper look to accentuate the connection to lightning and defined forms. This is a nod to its ruling planets of Uranus and Saturn. Aquarius is the sign at the midpoint between winter and spring in the northern hemisphere, and summer and autumn in the southern hemisphere. It carries the spark that quickens the beginning of life or the ripening of the seed. The glyph's two lines are separated by a gap, and this expresses the paradoxes and the polarities in the Aquarian psyche. Aquarius's search for resolution and synthesis is encoded in the glyph. All the air sign glyphs contain horizontal lines, because the winds circling the Earth touch everything; they carry sounds, humidity, scents, and spiritual influences to every place and person.

The crooked lines in the glyph tack back and forth, reaching toward each other and separating. This seeking never reaches a static conclusion as an Aquarian's exploration never ends. Use your imagination to see this glyph as a representation of how you have a relationship with all you observe in yourself and in society. The symmetry of the glyph also suggests the capacity to find a middle way between all seemingly opposed things. The empty path between the lines symbolizes the flow of consciousness and spirit you achieve when you are free and unbound.

By meditating on the glyph, you will develop a deeper understanding of what it is to be Aquarius. You may also come up with your own personal gnosis or story about the glyph that can be a key that is uniquely yours. The glyph for Aquarius can be used in a similar fashion to the scribing of an invoking pentacle that is used to open the gates to the elemental realms. However, instead of the elemental realms, this glyph opens the way to the realm of mind and spirit that is the source of Aquarius. To make this glyph work, you need to deeply ingrain the feeling of scribing this glyph. Visually, it is a simple glyph, so memorizing it is easy, but having a kinesthetic feel for it turns it into magick. Spend some time doodling the glyph on paper. Try drawing the glyph on your palm with a finger for several repetitions as that adds several layers of sensation and memory patterns.

Whenever you need access to more of your magickal energy, scribe the Aquarius glyph in your mind, on your hand, in the air—however you can. Then pull and channel the energy and feel your center fill with whatever you need. It takes very little time to open this connection using the glyph. Consider making this one of the practices you use to get ready to do divination, spell work, ritual, or just to start your day.

Aquarius Patterns

This is a short list of patterns, guidelines, and predilections for Aquarius Sun people to get you started. If you keep a book of shadows, or a journal, or files on a digital device to record your thoughts and insights on magickal work, you may wish to create your own list to expand upon these. The process of observing, summarizing, and writing down your own ideas in a list is a great way to learn about your sign.

⟳ The image associated with Aquarius is a person holding a pitcher or vase so that its contents are pouring out. Aquarius is an air sign, but that image and the name of the sign suggests water. Focus on the pitcher and what it represents. It is a tool that makes it easier to transport water—an idea made into a reality, which is the work of a fixed air sign.

⟳ Aquarius is the sign of civilization. Ideas organized into structures, whether they be philosophy, religion, ideology, technology, or science, fascinate the Aquarian mind.

◎ Aquarians want to be independent, and to do so, they must understand themselves. A great deal of your effort goes to determining which parts of you are social conditioning and which parts of you are truly inherent.

◎ Each Aquarius has a few contradictions and paradoxes in their core. Perhaps the most important of these is the need for personal independence and the need to belong to a group, organization, or movement. Balancing the personal and the societal is part of an Aquarian's life work.

◎ It is in exploring the interplay between your individuality and your membership in society where you discover insights that fuel your personal evolution; this eventually leads to changes in the world around you.

◎ There are many dualities in all the air signs, and in Aquarius, these are in a higher dynamic tension. Which is better, the wisdom of the past or the innovation of the future? Is it better to work from within a system or to overthrow it?

◎ Aquarius often has an odd relationship with time. Its original ruling planet was Saturn (Chronos), which rules linear time, and in modern times Uranus became Aquarius's ruler. Uranus shatters time and rules nonlinear time. In practical terms, this means Aquarians need to be mindful of tasks and schedules because their internal clock listens to both ruling planets.

◎ You like to bend rules, break rules, and make rules. Sometimes you are doing all three things at once.

◎ Aquarians can pretend to fit in and code switch to say and do things that make you look mainstream, but this takes a toll on you. You need to be your authentic, very nonstandard self regularly or it will sap your will to live.

◎ You tend to befriend the outcasts, the underdogs, the eccentrics, and the wild-eyed dreamers.

◎ When it comes to your aesthetics and sense of fashion, you will always stand out. Sometimes you will be ahead of your time, and sometimes you will be in another timeline in another reality. Be bold and be certain you are making the statement you want to in the moment.

◎ You can appear cold and detached when you are aiming for objectivity. Internally you are buzzing with emotions you'd rather not express.

◎ There is a strong Aquarian yearning to explore the edges of the known and of acceptability. You may look at the world with the perspective of an anthropologist or a visiting alien from another world.

◎ Like all air signs, you need regular mental stimulation to recharge yourself. Intelligent conversation with sincere people, quirky or edgy music, and art that operates on many levels are restorative for you.

◎ It is common for Aquarians to be described as progressive, and many are, but it isn't the most accurate way to describe them. Aquarians want to change the world and make it better from *their* perspective. For some Aquarians, *better* means returning to traditional values, and for others, it means forging a new path. This is a humanitarian urge at the level of systems rather than individuals.

☉ Aquarius is easily caught up in ideas and abstractions and loses track of the physical world. Form habits or friendships that drag you back to your physical senses so you can experience the beauty of the world. If you do this regularly, you will be happier.

Fixed Air

The four elements come in sets of three that repeat. The modalities known as cardinal, fixed, and mutable are three different flavors or styles of manifestation for the elements. The twelve-fold pattern that is the backbone of astrology comes from the twelve combinations produced from four elements times three modalities. As you go around the wheel of the zodiac, the

order of the elements is always fire, earth, air, then water, while the modalities are always in the order of cardinal, fixed, then mutable. Each season begins in the cardinal modality, reaches its peak in the fixed modality, and transforms to the next season in the mutable modality. The cardinal modality is the energy of creation bursting forth, coming into being, and spreading throughout the world. The fixed modality is the harmonization of energy so that it becomes and remains fully itself and is preserved. Fixed does not mean static or passive; it is the work of maintaining creation. The mutable modality is the energy of flux that is flexibility, transformation, death, and rebirth.

Aquarius is the eleventh sign in the zodiac, so it is air of the fixed modality. This is why an Aquarius witch can use their power of mind and imagination to manifest things, to make ideas into fixed realities. Although as an Aquarius witch you can call upon air in all its forms, it is easiest to draw upon fixed air.

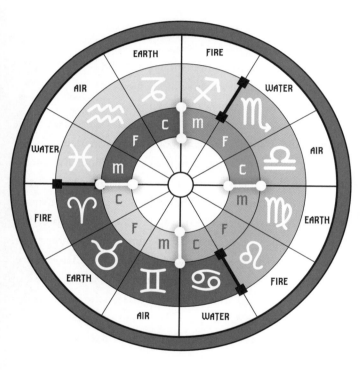

The elements and modalities on the wheel

Uranus, Your Ruling Planet

Your Sun sign determines the source and the type of energy you have in your core. The ruling planet for a sign reveals your go-to moves and your intuitive or habitual responses for expressing that energy. Your ruling planet provides a curated set of prebuilt responses and custom-tailored stances for you to use in day-to-day life. Uranus is the modern ruling planet for Aquarius with Saturn as the traditional ruler. If you want to know more about the mythological connections, look up Ouranos, Kronos, and Zeus. You'll find tales of rebellion, the overthrow of the old order, and creation born of destruction; all of these are Aquarian themes. If you only look at the old myths, it is a bit dire, so let's look at a modern story. The glyph for Uranus looks like the starship Enterprise from *Star Trek: The Next Generation*. Even if you're not familiar with Star Trek, you've probably heard the tagline: "To boldly go where no one has gone before." Uranus sponsors a desire to go beyond the known, shatter the known, and go beyond the speed of light.

Aquarius witches are more affected by whatever Uranus is doing in the heavens. It is useful to keep track of the aspects Uranus is making with other planets, especially Mercury. The same is true for Saturn to some degree. You will also have a boost of power when the Sun is in the same degree as Uranus or Saturn in your birth chart. You can get basic information on what aspects mean and when they are happening in astrological calendars and online resources. You will feel Uranus and Saturn retrogrades more strongly than most people, but you can make them useful periods to analyze what you've already done. Aquarius witches will notice that the impact of the Uranus retrograde will start earlier and end a few days later than the listed duration. When Saturn is in Aquarius, you will be more grounded and empowered for about two and a half years. This happens roughly every twenty-nine years. The first step to using the power of Uranus or Saturn is to pay attention to what it is doing, how you feel, and what is happening in your life.

Witches have the gift to shift their relationship with the powers they work with and the powers that influence them. As an Aquarius witch, you are connected to the power of Uranus. By paying close attention to how those energies affect you, it becomes possible to harness those energies to purposes you choose. Uranus can be as great a source of energy for an Aquarius witch as the element of air. Although there is some overlap between the qualities and capacities assigned to Uranus and air, the differences are much greater. Uranus shows you how you are inimitable and different from all others; it is the spark of individuality. Air provides the words, concept, and process that allows you to perceive and to express your uniqueness. Uranus is both the sky and the lightning bolt that briefly connects heaven and Earth to bring change. Air connects all that exists between heaven and Earth in an ongoing dialogue. Freewheeling Uranus and its tension with Saturn, the maker of rules, is the dynamo that powers the Aquarian personality. Air is the principle of agency, of interconnectedness, through which an Aquarius can express their power to have an impact on others. Over time, you can map out the overlapping regions and the differences between Uranus and air. Using both planetary and elemental resources can give you a much broader range and more finesse.

Aquarius and the Zodiacal Wheel

The order of the signs in the zodiac can also be seen as a creation story where the run of the elements repeats three times. Aquarius is in the final third of the zodiac, which is also the third appearance of the four elements in the story of the universe. Having experienced themselves, the goal of the elements at this point is to understand their relationship to the whole pattern. Aquarius remembers their purposes for coming into being. The air of Aquarius is focused on moving through the planes, earthward, to manifest ideals. As such, the air of Aquarius is the most tangibly influential of all the versions of the element of air.

Although true for all witches, the Aquarius witch needs to apply themselves to discovering who they are and what their role is in the physical and spiritual realms. When you can regularly connect with your ideals and your roles in the world, you become a conduit for your magick, and the people and projects that matter to you will thrive. This is the full expression of being in the final story arc of the zodiac. You can make progress in this quest through meditation and inner journeys, but that alone will not do. The Aquarius witch learns by exploring, imagining, thinking, debating, taking action, and repeating the process. Although Aquarians are sometimes stereotyped as being eccentric or too impractical, it is more accurate to say that they see a world many others can't see that is waiting to exist. They are experimenting to find new methods to foster its creation. When an Aquarius witch connects to the spiritual qualities of their air, they become a visionary and an implementer of the magick of the world.

The sign and planet rulers on the zodiac wheel

AQUARIUS
CORRESPONDENCES

Power: To Know

Keyword: Universality

Roles: Reformer, Futurist, Innovator

Ruling Planet: Uranus with secondary ruler Saturn

Element: Fixed Air

Colors: Magenta, Electric Blue, and Purple

Shape: Triangle

Metals: Aluminum, Uranium, and Lead

Body Part Ruled: Calves and Ankles

Day of the Week: Saturday

Affirmation:
I am whole unto myself, and
I am part of a greater wholeness.

WITCHCRAFT THAT COMES NATURALLY TO AN AQUARIUS

Mickie Mueller

The magickal abilities that seem to come naturally to an Aquarian witch is the aptitude to whip up magick intuitively on the fly using unexpected materials and methods. In my experience, our magickal style tends to be free-form and less structured. We're innovating, substituting ingredients, tools, and rewriting spells to suit us or just coming up with our own spur of the moment. We prefer doing things our way, which means that you probably won't even do things exactly as this book suggests. We're rebels, and we know it. We inhabit that space between air and water; we are practically liminal beings ourselves living between the worlds most of the time. If someone talks an elusive Aquarian into gathering with other witches and they need someone to hold a quarter in a ritual, monitor energies, or cast a quick but strong circle, an Aquarian witch can get that done like it's our full-time job. We're that Swiss army knife witch—point us where you need us, we'll make that happen, and we'll do it with flair!

Using our mind in our witchcraft is key and we love finding a new magickal perspective. Aquarians are likely to figure out some magickal correspondences others hadn't thought of. For example, I've assigned correspondences to rocks I've found on the ground based on where they were located, the shape, or even the mood I was in when I found them. Aquarians are likely to use many areas of academia for inspiration. Folklore, archaeology, plant remedies, philosophy, mythology, even science may be included as reference materials in some of our witchcraft. Yes, we love to innovate, but if we're looking back in time for our magick, we're going way back, because Aquarians seem to love learning about archaic methods for magick even if we're likely to update them. Witchcraft is unlimited when you're seeing the world through those Aquarian-colored glasses.

Psychic Skills and Divination

The first psychic skill I ever developed was psychic dreaming. As a child, I learned that occasionally I had dreams foretelling future events or tapped into things I didn't know about through other mundane methods. I also suffered from nightmares; likely the culmination of my childhood Aquarian concern about the world around me coupled with my imagination and creativity. I was still in grade school when I found a dream book in the Scholastic catalog that I ordered, devoured, and used to teach my Aquarian witchling mind how to analyze and track my dreams, look for patterns, and even develop some lucid dreaming skills to banish nightmares so I could get some rest.

Another psychic skill that dovetails with dream interpretation is augury. Learning the basic meanings of dream symbolism can also be helpful when interpreting signs that we might see in the waking world. I've always naturally looked for meaning in life events, chance meetings, an animal appearing at an unusual time, or even a key I find in the street. I wonder if other Aquarian witches have found this to be true for themselves too?

I've always been drawn to Ouija boards and pendulums; both have the energy of communication that may appeal to my Aquarian witch colleagues. While I know there are some fears around one or both, my logical Aquarian mind uses these as merely tools that connect with my own psychic abilities. My answers unfold by the swing of the pendulum or the slide of a planchette through the ideomotor response, which is a phenomenon that involves involuntary movement caused by the subconscious mind. When I suggest these tools to others, I do so with the caveat that if someone has fears surrounding either of these, I recommend that

33

they steer clear unless they work on analyzing and unlodging those fears first. As witches, the energy we put into something influences our experiences and outcomes.

As an artist, I tend to be visual; working with tarot and oracle decks has always appealed to me. It's no surprise that Pamela Colman Smith, the artist of the Rider-Waite-Smith tarot, that influential deck from the turn of the century, is a fellow Aquarian. I love the idea of a picture or a symbol having many deep meanings. Studying them in all their different interpretations and allowing the images to inspire my intuition is fascinating to me. I also know several Aquarians who are naturally drawn to astrology. Is there anything airier than the night sky itself? I have always enjoyed following my own horoscope and I grew up very fascinated by our solar system, constellations, and pondering the expanses of space. I also have dyslexia, dyscalculia, and ADHD, making the deeper study of astrology a bit challenging for me personally. I have, however, been learning more about it as part of my undaunted Aquarian witch journey, and although I probably won't be calculating charts anytime soon, I can now read an astrological calendar well enough to find meaning to boost my connection to my Aquarian witchcraft.

Among an Aquarian witch's senses is often the talent to pick up on energy changes in a room or an individual. We tend to lean toward an empathic style of psychic ability. Aquarians can also get in our heads quite a bit, so trusting our skills in this area comes down to learning how to spot the difference between intuition and anxiety—tricky! The best way for an Aquarian witch to tap into our intuition is to move our attention out of our heads for a few moments and discern what we sense in our own body about a space or person.

Aquarian Spellcrafting

So, what do the spells of an Aquarian witch look like? Our sacred spaces are probably unconventional in appearance. My husband never touches rocks on the bookshelf when cleaning without checking in with me first. "Is this just a rock, or is it part of a spell you've got going?" In fairness, it could be either. The Aquarian witchcraft altar might have an interesting, twisted root to represent a deity, or the shell of a weird, winged insect to represent the air element. Yes, there are rules, but they are our rules and subject to change when inspiration strikes.

Spell work is likely going to include big change work, whether it's internal work we're doing for ourselves or for others. We can be found doing spells for humanitarian causes, to help our communities, healing the planet, or justice. We tend to follow up these spells with some kind of real-world action.

We can personally benefit from doing magick surrounding inner journeys like shadow work. Getting in touch with our feelings after a lifetime of carrying the weight of the world can be very empowering for a brave Aquarian witch. We may be very interested in figuring out what makes our own brains tick because having agency over ourselves is very important.

We're also likely to cast spells for betterment of our own everyday lives; we love to have beauty around us, even if our view of beauty is unconventional. Our prosperity and abundance spells may lean toward boosting our finances in innovative ways through entrepreneurial enterprises rather than more standard flows of abundance like a nine-to-five button-down job.

Aquarian witches also do lots of work to shield our energy and the energy of our loved ones. Because we lean toward empathy and sensing shifts in others, we can also inadvertently absorb energy from our environment and the people we interact with. The good news is, we can usually also recognize when energy clearing is needed. Aquarian witches often spend some time and magickal energy keeping up with personal wards. Neglecting this work can leave us feeling anxious (but only deep down; others will never see it), so we work magick to protect our energy quite often just to keep things running smoothly in our lives.

My spells usually include stones and herbs of all varieties. I find that bringing earth energy in helps me stay grounded and focused on the task at hand. The truth is, as an Aquarian, I also love the pretty things! I often include candles in my spells. I enjoy the beautiful colors and shapes that candles come in; they make a spell into art. I especially love inscribing words and symbols into the wax, bringing the power of expression into the spell. I love to write my intentions out to burn; whether my goal is banishing what's on the paper or lovingly releasing it into the realm of spirit to manifest, I know that my approach will be aligned with my will. I speak out my incantations with a bellow, a whisper, or anything in between. The voice can be a powerful way for an Aquarian witch to raise energy for a spell. Sometimes my instinct about how to perform a spell is an important aspect of my process. As I'm gathering up supplies and flipping through books, I get flashes of inspiration, "Oh, that asafetida I just bought would be perfect, don't forget to grab that antique paperweight!" and I just go with it. In these moments, I can already feel the spell opening up to me.

Aquarian Witch Spell to Focus on a Task

As Aquarians, we often have too many interesting thoughts in our heads at one time and maybe a song as well, so getting an important task done can be a challenge. We certainly don't have a lack of imagination, we have too much. All that creative energy can make concentration difficult. I hope this spell helps you complete your missions large and small!

You will need:

+ Oil warmer/burner that holds water in the top and a tealight at the bottom
+ Bottle filled with water
+ Blue or white tealight candle
+ Ground allspice
+ 3 drops essential oil (rosemary, frankincense, peppermint, lemongrass, or any citrus)

Note: Frankincense is the only cat- and dog-safe oil on this list. If you have pets and prefer to use one of the others on this list, you can do the spell in a room where pet friends can't enter. Always use safety precautions when using essential oils.

Bonus points: Wear garnet, tiger's eye, or malachite jewelry

Instructions:

Summon up the spirit of Aquarius and trace the glyph in the air over the bottle of water. Pour the water in the top of the oil burner. Add three drops of essential oil in with the water. Inscribe an open eye on the top of the tealight candle as you repeat the phrase, "I'm focused on the task at hand," then sprinkle with a pinch of allspice. Put the candle in the bottom of the warmer and light it. Get some energizing music going and begin your task. See how much you can get done before you need to add a bit of water to the reservoir at the top. Keep going Aquarian witch, you've totally got this! When you finish the task or the candle burns out (whichever happens first), reward yourself with a break and do something you enjoy!

Archetypes and Deities

When we think of the archetypes of Aquarius, of course the image of the water bearer comes to mind. There are several deities, spirits, and figures of mythology who resonate with Aquarius energy. Just like anything else in your magick and life, these aren't the only spiritual allies an Aquarian witch can work with, these are just a few you might find interesting or notable.

Prometheus

This Greek titan can be embraced by Aquarian witches as he is credited in some legends as being the creator of humanity itself, forming humankind out of clay to be awakened to reason by the goddess Athena. Prometheus most famously stole fire from the gods to bring to humans, thus being the catalyst of civilization, including technology, arts, and sciences.

Hyas

Hyas was the son of Atlas and a descendant of Oceanus who was killed by the lion he was hunting. He was placed among the stars as the constellation Aquarius directly across from Leo. One sets in the west as the other rises in the east, thus keeping Hyas eternally safe from the lion that took his life.

Goddess and Saint Brigid

Brigid walks between the worlds of goddess and saint; the Irish loved her so dearly that when Christian missionaries came, the people refused to give her up, so now we also have a Saint Brigid. Her feast day is Imbolc, February 1–2, which is the midpoint of Aquarius season and a power day for Aquarian witches. She is also a goddess of inspiration, poetry, healing, hearth, and home.

Hapi

Hapi is the androgenous Egyptian deity of the Nile and is especially associated with the rising of the constellation Aquarius coinciding with annual flooding of the life-giving river. Hapi is shown with breasts and a large fertile belly but also a pharaoh's beard. Hapi is depicted carrying two vases, which regulate the water of the Nile, much like the two vessels we see in the Star tarot card. According to a translation of the astronomical ceiling Zodiac of Dendera, this is the deity who is depicted in the constellation of Aquarius.[2]

Athena

Athena was born fully formed and armored from Zeus's head. She is the Greek goddess of wisdom, the arts, technology, heroes, and war; the owl is her symbol. She is independent and

2. French archaeologist and Egyptologist François Auguste Ferdinand Mariette discovered the Zodiac of Dendera in 1820. Mariette recognized Hapi portrayed in constellation Aquarius on the bas-relief star map depicted on the ancient Egyptian ceiling.

inventive and is interested in civilization. Athena can remind us that we have many aspects; be careful to feed the ones you wish to nurture and use each aspect only when appropriate.

Saraswati

Saraswati is a goddess whose name comes from the Sanskrit root word *saras*, which means "pooling water" as she is associated with lakes, water, and rivers. Saraswati is independent and often defiant in stories about her. She values creativity, the arts and sciences, literature, and poetry and is portrayed playing a stringed instrument called a veena. Among her symbols are a white lotus, a peacock, and a swan.

The Star Card Ritual: Seeking Your Divine Spark

Danielle Dionne

The Star card in the tarot corresponds with Aquarius. It is sequentially the card following the Tower, which is associated with upheaval, sudden change, or destruction. This ritual can be used to seek out the Star's bright blessings of hope, renewal, inspiration, healing, and empowerment after or during troubled times. I held this ritual with close friends on my birthday and have since used it in my solitary practice when in need of illumination. What wisdom from the heavens will you draw down to illuminate your path on Earth?

You will need:
  + An altar set up with a Star tarot card and a candle
  + Two pourable vessels of water
  + An empty bowl and a bowl filled with earth

Instructions:

When everything is set up, enter ritual consciousness however you normally do, and then follow this guided meditation.

Relax and center yourself. See before you the World Tree standing in magnificence. Walking to the World Tree, smell the earth around you. Feel the gentle breeze on your face. Hear the wind in the leaves. With your hand upon the World Tree, set your intentions to visit the celestial heavens seeking the spark of divine wisdom or your own unique spark of illumination.

Make your way through an opening in the tree and see a spiraling staircase. You see a light above and begin spiraling up, perhaps on the wings of an animal ally or even floating to the great above. Make your way up to this brightly lit celestial space. You may find yourself sitting on clouds or perched atop the tree.

Beyond the brightness, see a galaxy of starlight, vast and cosmic. You feel connected to all and aware of your uniqueness at the same time. Ponder this Aquarian paradox. As you sit in this expansive state, you see starlight explode in the distance like fireworks. You watch as a spark falls directly toward you and feel it land upon your head. You feel it ignite as inspiration lights up your mind. Take this time to fully receive this divine spark and feel the illumination, blessing you with inspiration.

Take this spark back with you and begin to descend and return. Spiraling down, flying down, floating down the way you came. Return now to ritual consciousness. Bring your awareness back to your body, aware of your breath.

The Star card depicts a naked woman as water bearer. She is liminal between the heavens and Earth. She embodies as above, so below. Approach your altar, upon which sits the water vessels and two bowls. Bring forth your inspiration and state it aloud. In her likeness, take up each vessel of water and pour into the empty bowl and the bowl containing soil. Illuminate the candle on the altar. This flame represents your light and inspiration that you will bear into the world.

Gaze upon your work, now aflame with your divine spark. May your path be illuminated and may you light the way in darkness to inspire others. When the ritual is complete, pour water and earth onto the land and body of water you wish to bless, dispersing this energy out into the world. Release your sacred space and thank your spirits. So mote it be!

MAGICAL
CORRESPONDENCES
Mickie Mueller

There are some spells and magick that align well with an Aquarian witch's energy. This is by no means an exhaustive list, but inspiration to spark your imagination with a few tools, methods, and spells that are likely to click with your style. As an example, you might want to use storm energy to send healing to a past situation using your voice and some incense. Perhaps you'll use a written petition under a container of charged water from a bank to draw in money.

Types of Spellcraft

+ Incantations and spoken magic

+ Magickal brews

+ Sigils and symbols

+ Wind, storms, and weather

+ Written petitions

+ Creative visualization and dreamwork

Magical Tools

- Container of water
- Pen and paper or journal
- Feathers of water birds and shells
- Incense and sacred smoke
- Bells/singing bowl
- Voice and musical instruments

Magical Goals and Spell Ideas

- Humanitarian/activism
- Healing
- Protection and shielding
- Personal development
- Money and prosperity
- Sending energy to past or future

TIMING, PLACES, AND THINGS

Ivo Dominguez, Jr.

You've probably encountered plenty of charts and lists in books and online, cataloging which things relate to your Sun sign and ruling planet. There are many gorgeously curated assortments of herbs, crystals, music playlists, fashions, sports, fictional characters, tarot cards, and more that are assigned to your Sun sign. These compilations of associations are more than a curiosity or for entertainment. Correspondences are like treasure maps to show you where to find the type and flavor of power you are seeking. Correspondences are flowcharts and diagrams that show the inner occult relationship between subtle energies and the physical world. Although there are many purposes for lists of correspondences, there are two that are especially valuable to becoming a better Aquarius witch.

The first is to contemplate the meaning of the correspondences, the ways in which they reveal meaningful details about your Sun sign and ruling planet, and how they connect to you. This will deepen your understanding of what it is to be an Aquarius witch.

The second is to use these items as points of connection to access energies and essences that support your witchcraft. This will expand the number of tools and resources at your disposal for all your efforts.

Each of the sections in this chapter will introduce you to a type of correlation with suggestions on how to identify and use it. These are just starting points, and you will find many more as you explore and learn. As you broaden your knowledge, you may find yourself a little bit confused as you find that sources disagree on the correlations. These contradictions are generally not a matter of who is in error but a matter of perspective, cultural differences, and the intended uses for the correlations. Anything that exists in the physical world can be described as a mixture of all the elements, planets, and signs. You may be an Aquarian, but depending on the rest of your chart, there may be strong concentrations of other signs and elements. For example, if you find that a particular herb is listed as associated with both Aquarius and Taurus, it is because it contains both natures in abundance. In the cases of strong multiple correlations, it is important to summon or tune in to the one you need.

Times

You always have access to your power as an Aquarius witch, but there are times when the flow is stronger, readily available, or more easily summoned. There are sophisticated astrological methods to select dates and times that are specific to your birth chart. Unless you want to learn quite a bit more astrology or hire someone to determine these for you, you can do quite well with simpler methods. Let's look at the cycles of the solar year, the lunar month, and the hours of day-night rotation. When the Sun is in Aquarius, or the Moon is in Aquarius, or late in the small hours of the night, you are in the sweet spot for tuning in to the core of your power.

Aquarius season is roughly January 21–February 18, but check your astrological calendar or ephemeris to determine when it is for a specific year in your time zone. The amount of accessible energy is highest when the Sun is at the same degree of Aquarius as it is in your birth chart. This peak will not always be on your birth date, but very close to it. Take advantage of Aquarius season for working magick and for recharging and storing up energy for the whole year.

The Moon moves through the twelve signs every lunar cycle and spends around two and half days in each sign. When the Moon is in Aquarius, you have access to more lunar power because the Moon in the heavens has a resonant link to the Sun in your birth chart. At some point during its time in Aquarius, the Moon will be at the same degree as your Sun. For you, that will be the peak of the energy during the Moon's passage through Aquarius that month. While the Moon is in Aquarius, your psychism is stronger, as is your ability to manifest things. When the Moon is a waxing crescent in any sign, you can draw upon its power more readily because it is resonant to your sign.

The Sun enters Aquarius in winter in the northern hemisphere. The peak of Aquarius season is its midpoint at the fifteenth degree; this is a special day of power for you. It is also the astrological date for Imbolc, Candlemas, Brigid, or whatever name you use for this cross-quarter holiday. You can look up when the Sun is in the fifteenth degree of Aquarius for the current or future years using online resources or an ephemeris. Aquarius is the eleventh sign of the zodiac, and the zodiac is like a clock for the purposes of spell work. Late night corresponds to the airy power of Aquarius. If you are detail focused, you might be wondering when late night is. This varies with the time of year and with your location, but if you must have a time, think of it as 2:00 a.m. to 4:00 a.m. Or use your intuition for what constitutes late in the night. The powers that flow during this time are rich, creative, and filled with possibilities for you to experience. Plan on using the Aquarian energy of the deep of night to fuel and feed spells for communication, enlightenment, transformation, and pathfinding.

The effect of these special times can be joined in any combination. For example, you can choose to do work late at night when the Moon is in Aquarius, or when the Sun is in Aquarius late at night, or when the Moon is in Aquarius during Aquarius season. You can combine all three as well. Experiment and use your instincts to discover how to use these in your work.

We are in the process of entering the Age of Aquarius, which is a complicated topic deserving a whole book of exploration. For approximately the next two thousand years, the background energy of the world will always have Aquarian qualities. This will be beneficial and challenging for all Aquarius witches. You will be more affected by the changes and transformations in the broader world. This gives you insights. You will also have a greater inherent capacity to make a difference in yourself and in society. This gives you power. And together, this results in greater personal accountability.

Places

There are activities, professions, phenomena, and behaviors that have an affinity, a resonant connection, to Aquarius and its ruling planet, Uranus. These activities occur in the locations that suit or facilitate their expressions. There is magick to be claimed from those places that is earmarked for Aquarius or your ruling planet of Uranus. Just like your birth chart, the world around you contains the influences of all the planets and signs, but in different proportions and arrangements. You can always draw upon Aquarius or Uranus or Saturn energy, though there are times when it is more abundant depending on astrological considerations. Places and spaces have energies that accumulate and can be tapped as well. Places contain the physical, emotional, and spiritual environments that are created by the actions of the material objects, plants, animals, and people occupying those spaces. Some of the interactions between these things can generate or concentrate the energies and patterns that can be used by Aquarius witches.

If you search in astrology books, you'll find listings of places assigned to Aquarius and Uranus that include locations such as these:

- ◎ Any place during a thunderstorm
- ◎ Aboard any vehicle that flies or hovers
- ◎ Cyberspace, virtual realms, telepresence meetings
- ◎ Avant-garde events, music and art festivals, scenes such as Burning Man
- ◎ Conventions, both serious and playful

These are very clearly linked to the themes associated with Aquarius and Uranus. With a bit of brainstorming and free-associating, you'll find many other less obvious locations and situations where you can draw upon this power. For example, an immersive multimedia art show, a protest, a public hearing, or a game online with friends can produce a current you can plug into. Any mentally stimulating activity connected to your ideology or causes—volunteering in a membership organization, writing a manifesto, networking for work or play, or similar activities—can become a source of power for an Aquarius witch. All implements or actions related to communication, technology, politics, or self-expression, as well as many more situations, also could be a source for energy.

While you can certainly go to places that are identified as locations where Aquarius and/or Uranus's energy is plentiful to do workings, you can find those energies in many other circumstances. Don't be limited by the idea that the places must be the ones that have a formalized link to Aquarius. Be on the lookout for Aquarius or Uranus themes and activities wherever you may be. Remember that people thinking, feeling, or participating in activities connected to your sign and its ruling planet are raising power. If you can identify with it as resonating with your Sun sign or ruling planet, then you can call the power and put it to use. You complete the circuit to engage the flow with your visualization, intentions, and actions.

Plants

Aquarius is airy, sparkly, zesty, and arranges things to maximize contrast, impact, or shock value. Uranus adds a focus on stimulating the mind and senses, having a sudden appeal or affect, and intensifying colors. Herbs, resins, oils, fruits, vegetables, woods, and flowers that strongly exhibit one or more of these qualities can be called upon to support your magick. Here are a few examples:

- ◎ Star anise to inspire your next great innovation.
- ◎ Valerian because it helps soothe an overactive nervous system.
- ◎ Cacao to lighten your mood and increase blood circulation.
- ◎ The zest of any type of citrus to clear the mind.
- ◎ Coffee, tea, or yerba maté to speed your thoughts.

Once you understand the rationale for making these assignments, the lists of correspondences will make more sense. Another thing to consider is that each part of a plant may resonate more strongly with a different element, planet, and sign. Vervain shows its connection with Aquarius and Uranus through its bright blue or purple flowers and its use as an aid to break obsession and overthinking. However, vervain is also used as an herb of Jupiter and Sagittarius for guidance to stay on track with the right action. Which energy steps forward depends on your call and invitation. "Like calls to like" is a truism in witchcraft. When you use your Aquarius nature to make a call, you are answered by the Aquarius part of the plant.

Plant materials can take the form of incense, anointing oils, altar pieces, potions, washes, magickal implements, foods, flower arrangements, and so on. The mere presence of plant material that is linked to Aquarius or Uranus will be helpful to you. However, to gain the most benefit from plant energy, you need to actively engage with it. Push some of your energy into the plants and then pull on it to start the flow. Although much of the plant material you work with will be dried or preserved, it retains a connection to living members of their species. You may also want to reach out and try to commune with the spirit, the group soul, of the plants to request their assistance or guidance. This will awaken the power slumbering in the dried or preserved plant material. Spending time with living plants, whether they be houseplants, in your yard, or in a public garden, will strengthen your conversation with the green beings under Aquarius's eye.

Crystals and Stones

Before digging into this topic, let's clear up some of
the confusion around the birthstones for the signs
of the zodiac. There are many varying lists for
birthstones. Also be aware that some are related to
the calendar month rather than the zodiacal signs. There
are traditional lists, but the most commonly available lists for
birthstones were created by jewelers to sell more jewelry. Also
be cautious of the word *traditional* as some jewelers refer to
the older lists compiled by jewelers as "traditional." The traditional lists created by magickal practitioners also diverge
from each other because of cultural differences and the avail-
ability of different stones in the times and places
the lists were created. If you have already formed
a strong connection to a birthstone that you
discover is not really connected to the energy
of your sign, keep using it. Your connection is
proof of its value to you in moving, holding,
and shifting energy, whether or not it is specifi-
cally attuned to Aquarius.

These are my preferred assignments of birthstones for
the signs of the zodiac:

Aries	Bloodstone, Carnelian, Diamond
Taurus	Rose Quartz, Amber, Sapphire
Gemini	Agate, Tiger's Eyes, Citrine
Cancer	Moonstone, Pearl, Emerald
Leo	Heliodor, Peridot, Black Onyx
Virgo	Green Aventurine, Moss Agate, Zircon
Libra	Jade, Lapis Lazuli, Labradorite
Scorpio	Obsidian, Pale Beryl, Nuummite
Sagittarius	Turquoise, Blue Topaz, Iolite
Capricorn	Black Tourmaline, Howlite, Ruby
Aquarius	Amethyst, Sugalite, Garnet
Pisces	Ametrine, Smoky Quartz, Aquamarine

There are many other possibilities that work just as well, and I suggest you find what responds best for you as an individual. I've included all twelve signs in case you'd like to use the stones for your Moon sign or rising sign. Hands-on experimentation is the best approach, so I suggest visiting crystal or metaphysical shops and rock and mineral shows when possible. Here's some information on the three I prefer for Aquarius.

Amethyst

Amethyst comes in many hues of violet, purple, and lilac. It has a long history of use in magick and spell work in many cultures. It opens the third eye and also opens a connection to higher consciousness. It is also known as the stone of sobriety, but this is not just about alcohol and abstinence. Amethyst has the capacity to tone down the excesses of strong emotion, of being trapped in looping thoughts, or anything else that impairs judgment. For Aquarius, it is also a stone for dreaming and visioning without fear. Amethyst also boosts both the physical and spiritual immune system.

Sugilite

This stone helps bring balance between head and heart, the individual and the collective, and other dualities that are Aquarian themes. Sugilite is nurturing and gentle in its approach to revealing the options and tasks at hand. This stone also helps encourage your body to connect with the pattern of its ideal form to encourage health. Aquarians sometimes have difficulty sharing their heart and deep emotions. Sugilite helps open and maintain emotional exchanges. Conversely, it is useful for cutting and releasing unwanted emotional attachments with integrity. For Aquarius, the best colors for this stone are purple or magenta.

Garnet

All the many types of garnet are good for Aquarians, but andradite garnet and grossular garnet are the best. These stones bring grounding and practicality to the more radical or risky plans that Aquarians tend to try. Garnets also activate resourceful thinking that can convert the unworkable into a reasonable option. These stones can rekindle passion and drive when you are feeling that you have gone cold. Garnet is also a helper when you are feeling alienated or out of touch with your magick and spiritual nature. This crystal's name comes from the Latin word for *pomegranate*. Look up pomegranate's mythic associations to know more about this stone.

Intuition and spiritual guidance play a part in the making of correlations and, in the case of traditional lore, the collective experience of many generations of practitioners. There is also reasoning behind how these assignments are made and understanding the process will help you choose well. Here are some examples of this reasoning.

◎ Crystals assigned to Aquarius are intense, vibrant colors because they suggest Aquarius and Uranus in their appearance. Bismuth crystals, star sapphires, and cavansite are good examples.

◎ Aquarius's metal is aluminum, and stones that have significant amounts of aluminum, such as kyanite, spinel, and alexandrite, also work well for you. Xenotime crystals contain traces of uranium, which is also associated with Aquarius.

◎ Crystals such as moldavite, tiger's eye, black onyx, and Herkimer diamond whose lore and uses are related to Aquarius or Uranus actions or topics, such as transformation, independence, and creativity, are recommended as crystals for Aquarius.

◎ Crystals that are the opposite of the themes for Aquarius provide a counterbalance to an excessive manifestation of Aquarius traits. For example, amber, morganite, and rose quartz are good for toning down the mind and amping up the heart.

◎ Crystals suggested for Leo, your opposite sign, are also useful to maintain your balance.

Working with Ritual Objects

A substantial number of traditions or schools of witchcraft use magickal tools that are consecrated to represent and hold the power of the elements. Oftentimes in these systems, there is one primary tool for each of the elements and other tools that are alternatives to these or are mixtures of elements. There are many possible combinations and reasons for why the elements are assigned to different tools in different traditions, and they all work within their own context. Find and follow what works best for you.

Magickal tools and ritual objects are typically cleansed, consecrated, and charged to prepare them for use. In addition to following whatever procedure you may have for preparing your tools, add in a step to incorporate your energy and identity as an Aquarius witch. This is especially productive for magickal tools and ritual objects that are connected to air or are used for centering work or to store or focus power. By adding Aquarius energy and patterning into the preparation of your tools, you will find it easier to raise, move, and shape energy with them in your workings.

There are many magickal tools and ritual objects that do not have any attachment to specific elements. The core of your life force and magickal power springs from your Aquarius Sun. So, when you consciously join your awareness of your Aquarius core with the power flowing through the tools or objects, it increases their effectiveness. Develop the habit of using the name *Aquarius* as a word of power, the glyph for Aquarius for summoning power, and the vibrant violet and electric blue colors of Aquarius to visualize its flow. Whether it be a pendulum, a wand, a crystal, or a chalice, your Aquarius energy will be quick to rise and answer your call.

A Charging Practice

When you consciously use your Aquarius witch energy to send power into tools, it tunes them more closely to your aura. Here's a quick method for imbuing any tool with your Aquarius energy.

1. Place the tool in front of you on a table or altar.
2. Take a breath in, imagining that you are breathing in electric blue energy, and then say "Aquarius" as you exhale. Repeat this three times.
3. If possible, while seated, reach down and touch your shins or calves with your fingertips. Then bring up your hands in front of you and hold them palms down, parallel and over each other with a gap of a few inches between them. Move your hands to the left as far as is comfortable. Now see your hands glowing blue. Move them together slowly to the right while also moving in a zigzag. You've just formed the glyph for Aquarius and

connected with the part of the body Aquarius rules.

4. Now, using your fingers, trace the glyph of Aquarius over or on the tool you are charging. Repeat this several times and imagine the glyph being absorbed by the tool.

5. Pick up the tool, take in a breath while imaging electric blue energy, and blow that charged breath over the tool.

6. Say "Blessed be!" and proceed with using the tool or putting it away.

Hopefully this charging practice will inspire you and encourage you to experiment. Feel free to use these spontaneously in all your workings. Whether it be a pendulum, a wand, a crystal, a chalice, a ritual robe, or anything else that catches your imagination, these simple methods can have a large impact. The Aquarius energy you imprint into them will be quick to rise and answer your call.

HERBAL
CORRESPONDENCES

These plant materials all have a special connection
to your energy as an Aquarius witch. There are many
more, but these are a good starting point.

Herbs

Spikenard	for devotion and a higher perspective
Witch hazel	for finding your path or answers
Linden	protection, justice, and peace

Flowers

Malva Zebrina	for soothing stress or calling passion
Orchid	attracts love and prosperity
Bird-of-paradise	stimulates creativity and insight

Incense and Fragrances

Neroli	to protect your aura and magick
Allspice	to keep you energized and on task
Wisteria	for psychic development and wisdom

CLEANSING AND SHIELDING

Mickie Mueller

All witches should have some practices they use to keep the energy in their lives running smoothly, and Aquarian witches are no exception. Whether it's your personal vibrancy or the energy of the spaces you're inhabiting regularly like home, office, or even your car, you need to keep up your energetic hygiene. Keeping a handle on the spiritual forces around you will help you stay true to your magick and keep your energy from misfiring as you navigate your witchcraft journey and life in general. When things feel like they're not flowing, a full cleansing and shielding practice can get everything unstuck and moving again.

When and Where Are Extra Precautions Needed?

Personal shielding is very important to us because we're in touch with our interconnectedness to all things, so when vibrations are off, we really feel it. A big concert, party, weekend festival, or convention can be our jam, but being in crowds of people for long periods can leave us with too much sensory and psychic input. Exposure to petty gossip, navigating small talk, and societal niceties can leave us questioning ourselves and working extra hard on every interaction, leaving us overburdened with too much psychic sludge. I like to wear protective amulets when going out to help keep toxic energy at bay. I have many pieces that serve this purpose, but an amethyst or garnet piece can help you access Aquarian witch energy to add an extra layer of protection. I also have added a drop of protective essential oil to hand sanitizer that I keep hanging on my purse. It allows me to instantly cleanse away things untoward, both physical and spiritual. If you do this, make sure you check how much to dilute the oil for safety.

Another situation that can mess with an Aquarian witch's energy is working or living in a space where someone is trying to control us. Anyone who tries to make an Aquarian conform or attempts to reel in our independent nature is barking up the wrong tree. Yes, we can be obstinate and opinionated, but that aspect of our nature really gets activated when someone tries to micromanage us or tell us what to do, leaving us feeling all irritated and making it harder for us to access our problem-solving and innovative strengths. Try wearing an oil that's citrus based and mixed with a carrier oil or add a few drops to a bottle of Moon water and use it as a body spray. This can perform double duty of protection from overbearing energy, plus it can help keep your mind clear to better navigate those interactions with grace and cool, calm diplomacy. A few rowanberries in a pocket charm bag is another trick I've used. Rowan is the Celtic tree associated with the goddess Brigid and offers protection from all forms of negative and controlling energy.

We love our tech, but too much social media or news isn't good for anyone. Both are designed to easily engage a curious and nontraditional mind like ours into getting stuck scrolling for much longer than we intend. Yes, we can come off as unemotional to others, but some of those news stories and social media battles with trolls can really get into our psyche and be quite painful. I like to tuck a drawing of a protective sigil facing the back of my phone backed by a piece of aluminum foil to reflect negativity back to the source and hold it in place with my phone case. You can try the King Solomon sixth pentacle of Saturn, fifth pentacle of the Moon, or create your own sigil customized for your needs or tradition.

These are some situations that can really cause our energy to fizzle, feel weighed down, or just get stuck and in need of some energetic housekeeping. I always remind people that another thing that can throw our energies off is ourselves. It's important to recognize that negativity doesn't always only come from an outside source; just like in a scary movie, sometimes the call is coming from inside the house. Doing our inner work can help that happen less often, but it can still happen to anyone because healing ourselves from our own inner shadows is ongoing work. The results of that introspection can benefit from clearing and cleansing work as we release unwanted social conditioning and reveal our true selves. Regardless of where it originated, the same rituals will take care of the problem.

I'll share my Aquarius witch version of my go-to rituals for cleansing and shielding that you can use yourself. Of course, feel free to adjust these rituals to suit your needs, tradition, and what you have on hand. I recommend that you always do cleansing first and then follow it up with shielding. There's no point adjusting the energies in your life without following it up with wards, that way your hard work will last much longer and be much more effective.

It should be said that before undertaking spiritual cleansing, physical cleaning should take place. Astral nasties can get snagged up in dirty carpets or hole up among clutter, so removing those obstacles first sets you up for success.

House Cleansing Practice

I like to ritually cleanse my space first and myself afterward. Much in the way you can get dirty hands doing physical cleaning, it makes sense to do that work and then follow it up with cleansing your personal energy. For this ritual, we'll use the energy of air and expression to blow out the psychic cobwebs from our space. As an Aquarian witch, all the airy forms of cleansing have extra power when wielded by you.

You will need:

+ An instrument or noisemaker of your choice
+ Sacred smoke

Instructions:

Instruments for this can include bells, singing bowls, a drum, an electric guitar, or a big pasta pot turned upside down and a wooden spoon to bang on it! Whatever style fits your personal taste. As for smoke, I like to use stick incense or cones in a scent like frankincense, lavender, an Aquarius blend, or any form of sacred smoke you prefer. An alternative to smoke is a homemade spray. Simply add a few drops of airy

essential oils that correspond with clearing and purification to a small mister bottle of water. You can try
oils like frankincense, lavender, pine, or mint. Top it off
with a splash of spirits like vodka or isopropyl alcohol
if you'll be saving it for future use.

An Aquarian witch can easily work influential
magic with the power of our own breath, our voice,
and our words. I will include an incantation that you
may use as is, or feel free to embellish it, change it
around, write your own, or speak (or think) your
own words from the heart in the moment.

Take a beat to center your energy by focusing
on your breath; I like box breathing. Breathe in four
counts, hold four counts, breathe out four counts,
hold four counts. Repeat four times. Now, beginning
at your front door, play your instrument joyously.
As you ring your bells, bang the pot, or shred some
licks on your guitar, do it with intention and imagine it reverberating through your space, raising all
the frequencies to match your objective and chasing
lower frequencies out. Do this in every room in your
house, ending by opening your back door so that low-
frequency energies can escape from your cacophony

of good energy! Follow the same path you took with your music using your sacred smoke (or spray) and allow the scents to dance in the air in each room as you repeat the following incantation or one of your own. Say it with all the strength you have attached to the words; this incantation isn't a request, it's a firmly stated declaration of fact. Tone matters here.

I clean and clear this space of all that does not align with my own highest purpose. This space is mine. I determine the energy that resides here. Any nasties that linger, you are not welcome, you are compelled to hit the road and may never return. By the power of my sovereign self, an Aquarian witch, standing in my truest power and fortified by my spiritual allies, I declare this space clear.

Afterward, play some of your favorite music throughout the house.

Water Bearer's Clearing and Protection

After a house cleansing, I like to do a personal cleansing using this method. Fill your tub with bathwater. If you wish, you can bring in the same incense or spray you used in the house cleansing ritual. You can add a half cup of salt of your choice to the water. I use a mix of sea salt and Epsom salt. Epsom salt is a naturally occurring compound made of three elements: magnesium (for healing), sulfur (destroying hexes), plus oxygen (air element). I also recommend orange or lemon peels and a few drops of energy-clearing and protective essential oils like chamomile, lavender, or my new Aquarian witch favorite, neroli; I use all three.

If you don't have a tub, you can add a few drops of essential oils and a pinch of salt to your favorite bodywash and scrub yourself down in the shower. Whether using the shower or bath method, imagine the spirit of Aquarius pouring cleansing water from the stars over you. Imagine it filling your tub or shower with glowing water purifying everything it touches, dissolving whatever doesn't serve you. The contents of Aquarius's vase will leave you shielded with transparent armor so that no low-vibration energy can penetrate. Even if you have a tub, you can still enchant some bodywash as I described and use it every time you shower using the Aquarius vase visualization to keep your shield constantly refreshed. Wearing protective jewelry or oils can add an extra layer of protection whenever you need it.

Warding Your Home

Now that you've cleared the energy of your space, you'll need to put some magickal wards in place to maintain the energy you worked so hard to transform. I start with magickally sealing the doors and windows. Use a small dish of water and add one to two drops of protective oil; try neroli or any citrus. Lavender has also worked well for me. You might try an Aquarius blend like Ivo's Aquarius Anointing Oil Recipe on page 213. Simply dip your finger in the water and draw a protective sigil, rune, or other symbol on every door and window in the house. A pentagram is classic, but you can also use an equal-arm cross, the ogham for rowan, or any other protective symbol that resonates with you. Draw the Aquarius glyph on the window or door just above it to symbolize the power of Aquarius, adding spiritual energy to the protective symbol. I visualize the symbols repeating all over the walls like the cascading code in the film *The Matrix*.

After you've sealed the doors and windows, you can add some extra wards, such as a set of wind chimes outside charged to break up psychic attacks before they can get in. Small mirrors like round or square one-inch mirrored tiles are perfectly aligned with Aquarian magick. Place mirrors in windows strategically to reflect negativity back to the sender. Modern mirrors are made by bonding aluminum to the back of glass and aluminum is an Aquarian metal with the magickal powers of protection, boosting mental abilities and balancing energies.

Make a brew of Aquarian protective herbs in hot water like you would a tea. You can use any or all of the following: linden flowers, dandelion, chamomile, lavender, mint, or rue. Once cool, strain through a coffee filter and mix it half and half with white vinegar in a spray bottle. This wash can be used to clean all the mirrors physically and spiritually in your house and simultaneously charge them as protective wards. If you love this idea, you can learn more about the history, folklore, and how to use mirrors in my book *The Witch's Mirror*.

WHAT SETS AN AQUARIUS OFF, AND HOW TO RECOVER

Mickie Mueller

Life is full of things that irritate us, but for every poison, there is a remedy, and it's often closer than you expect. You might already know that if you find the irritating plant poison ivy growing in the woods, its natural remedy, jewelweed, is likely growing nearby. Similarly, we'll notice certain irritating situations getting on our last nerve, but when we connect with our Aquarian witch energy, we also have traits to help us learn from and overcome the things that activate our annoyance. Let's commiserate over a few sources of frustration and discover the jewels of our Aquarian witch powers to help us regain our composure and come back to center.

An Ill Wind Is Blowing

Gossip is the energy of air used in a negative and petty way; as a fixed air sign, it's a big irritant. Integrity in communication is important to us. I've discovered that people who badmouth others to me are usually gossiping about me to others as well, and it's not a good look. When someone comes to me with this behavior, I can't stand it when they try dragging me into their drama. Honestly, I have many other subjects I'd rather discuss than spreading or receiving rumors. When gossips show up in my life, I've learned to hold my cards close and never reveal anything to them that I wouldn't want broadcasted publicly.

The jewels we possess for dealing with this irritant are our compassionate diplomacy and our stubbornness, which we can call upon when dealing with a gossip. Keeping emotions out of the equation is the best way to set a boundary. We can simply stop the person who's getting started on a big juicy bit of slander by making a firm but calm statement delivered in a nonconfrontational tone such as, "Oh, I should stop you there. I've made a personal commitment not to discuss people's private business when they aren't present themselves. If you have questions or concerns that you want to help them with, I bet they would rather have you discuss that with them privately." After that, if they try to push the story on you further, stand your ground with a broken record tactic by reminding them, "Again, I've made a commitment to myself not to talk about people when they're not present, perhaps you can help me with that by bringing your concerns to them instead." The request for their help can really shift the conversation. If they continue, you can add a shutdown statement like, "I'm sure you don't intend to gossip." (Which sounds like a statement but is intended as a suggestion.) And then change the subject.

Spell to Halt Gossip

This is a simple pen-and-paper spell. Use this one when the gossip is about you or a loved one whom you have permission to work magick for. Write the gossip's name on a small slip of paper three times in three separate rows. Over the top of each name, write, "Keep my name out of your mouth," or alter the phrase to suit your needs. Then draw a square around the whole thing to illustrate your control over your own story. Burn the paper in a fireproof dish. I've had a gossip stop completely after this step. To add power to this spell, save the ashes for the next windy day and scatter them with the wind at your back.

I Won't Do What You Tell Me

We hate being told what to do. The best way to get an Aquarian to do something is to tell us not to, or that we can't. We value our liberty, so if someone tries to use a heavy hand and push us in their direction, that's a big irritant and we're likely to just go ahead and do the opposite of that. When it comes to personal freedom, my money is on the Aquarian every time. I have literally done things just because someone tried to force me to do the opposite, and refused to do something that another person suggested would be for my best interests. Sometimes this contrarian attitude has been to my own detriment. Let's unpack this irritant and see if there's a different Aquarian way to handle it.

Curiosity and critical thinking are the jewels that can help us separate our reaction from facts. We can ask ourselves, Why am I so opposed to the suggestion? Is it just a kneejerk reaction? Sometimes I take advice; I'll often listen to an expert or take a recommendation from a trusted friend. If I'm feeling spikey about what someone wants me to do, it's often the delivery of the "suggestion" that I'm opposed to. This is a moment when I've learned I can tap into my Aquarian curiosity and love of research. If you find yourself in this situation, first step back from it and investigate the validity of the suggestion using critical thinking and legitimate sources. Is it based on evidence? Are you opposed to the advice based on a bad experience, your personal thoughts about the person suggesting it, or their overbearing delivery? See if you can separate the message from the messenger. Being bossy is a trap we can fall into ourselves, so when we see it in others, we really reject it. Once we do a deep dive, if we find out that it was a bad suggestion, we can discard the idea with a clear conscience because we have the "receipts." If we discover that it was a good suggestion, well, after all your research, it's become at least partly your idea, so you can proceed with facts to back it up.

Quickie Meditation to Call Back Your Energy

Interactions with domineering people who aren't aligned with our personal mission can be more than annoying, they can be spiritually draining. Let's draw back our personal power. Close your eyes and do some deep breathing, relaxing your body and allowing any random thoughts to float by like clouds in the wind. Acknowledge them and release them. Imagine a chalice above your head glowing softly. This vessel is like a magnet, and the only thing it attracts is your own energy. Now you imagine stars being pulled in from far and wide toward the gently glowing chalice. The stars are little bits of personal energy you've lost or left behind during the course of life and its challenges; each one is purified by the wind blowing across them. They're drawn into the top of the chalice; as the chalice fills with your bits of wayward energy, it glows brighter and brighter. At last, the chalice tips and pours its contents into the top of your head. Feel it filling your body from your head to your feet with energy you've lost and welcome it back. When the meditation is finished, give thanks and take a deep breath, returning to regular consciousness.

If It's a War You Want

Personal confrontations are the worst. Fighting against societal structures might be right in an Aquarian witch's wheelhouse, but gearing up for a one-on-one battle isn't something we relish at all, even when it's necessary. Why is that? Well, it's bound to get emotional, and that feels really uncomfortable; we tend to take criticism to heart, and we really dislike hurting other people. Confrontations are a big irritant that I can almost physically feel in my skin. Do you feel that way too? I can't tell you how many times I've banged out an angry yet well-thought-out response to something I've seen on social media only to take a deep breath and delete it before posting. I had good points, but the thought of engaging in the personal battle that would probably ensue was just too exhausting, especially when tone is so hard to express online. Sometimes we have no choice but to have a conversation about difficult feelings or situations and hash things out. Don't. Want. To.

Communication and emotional detachment are the Aquarian jewels that can shine in this instance. Not taking things personally is a great tool for talking things through when going into an emotionally charged situation. Realizing that the other person's opinions and assumptions have nothing to do with you but are the result of the lens they see the world through is the key to getting to the bottom of relationship difficulties. Your perspective is probably a reflection of your own biases and experiences as well, so trying to look past your assumptions and asking questions while being clear about what you need might just change the tone of the interaction. If you can't come to a resolution, not taking it personally can help ease your own pain at the very least after the dust settles.

Time Travel Mental Practice for Calming Tempers

If you know the place where a big discussion is planned, you can picture the room in your head. If it's a place you're not familiar with, just imagine four walls and name it "the meeting place." Imagine you and the other person or people who will be having the discussion are in the room, frozen in time, no negative emotions, a clean conversational slate. Picture the room filled with light; send words into the light in that room, such as, "mutual understanding, open communication, reflection, calm," and allow those words and the energy behind them to circulate through the light in the room. Focus on this for as long as you feel necessary. If you're not good at picturing things in your head, you can draw a square with the names of everyone involved in the upcoming conversation inside of it as a place to focus your energy. You can even write the positive words over the top of the paper. In this way, you've used your Aquarian ability to step beyond time and set up the room to be a conducive space for open communication in advance.

Summoning Serenity: Crafting Incense and Conjuring Cool Spirits

Silver Daniels

Aquarians are famously known for their imaginative and inventive minds. Constantly exploring the depths of possibility, we tend to spend a lot of time in our own headspace. But sometimes, too much overthinking can get us into trouble, leading us astray from reality or even causing mental exhaustion. So, for all you creative thinkers looking for an escape from cerebral chaos, this incense recipe might be just what you need to keep your cosmic thoughts under control, allowing you to bask peacefully in the wonders of your imagination.

You will need:

Dry ingredients:

+ 10 grams lavender buds
+ 3 grams pinyon pine resin
+ ½ square camphor tablet

Wet ingredients:

+ 30 drops lavender essential oil
+ 15 drops lemon essential oil
+ ¼ teaspoon honey

Instructions:

When the Moon is waxing, pulverize the dry ingredients into a fine powder with a mortar and pestle. Next, moisten the powder with the wet ingredients.

Carefully mix until all ingredients are combined, ensuring your mixture has a malleable yet slightly sticky consistency. Then, transfer the mixture into a glass mason jar with an airtight lid.

Calling the Cool Spirits

Perform the conjuring with a lit wooden match, using the flame to trace the sign of the cross over sweet-smelling incense. While doing so, recite an appropriate conjuration that invokes spirits of peace and clarity. For example:

> Cooling spirits, I conjure thee to share your calm and
> coolness with me.
> By your grace and charity, may this incense bring me
> clarity.

Drop the lit match into the jar and immediately screw on the airtight lid. The flame will vanish and leave behind smokey tendrils—a sign that spirits are present. This cross-and-conjure method draws spirits into the container and binds them to work on infusing the incense with the requested qualities. A secure seal keeps these conjured spirits bound until the work is complete.

Set the jar on your altar and cover it with a clean white cloth to allow the spirits to work privately and peacefully. Next, light a tealight candle and set it atop the jar as an act of service to the energies you have employed, giving them the necessary light and strength to work on your behalf. For optimal potency, light a new candle periodically (at least once a week) over the course of twenty-one days to keep the spirits active and give the incense blend time to mature before use. Once the blend has cured, uncover the jar and remove the lid and release the spirits gracefully. Show appreciation for their hard work by offering them the first pinch of the incense and setting it alight so they can delight in its wonderful aroma.

Congratulations! You now have a carefully crafted incense enriched by spirits. Use it to bring a refreshing clarity into your mind and ease any anxieties or stress that might be holding you back from achieving peak focus.

PAMELA "PIXIE" COLMAN SMITH: AN ICONIC BUT ALMOST-FORGOTTEN AQUARIAN ARTIST

* * *

Alexandra Nic Bhé Chuille

Pamela "Pixie" Colman Smith is most often remembered as the artist behind the Rider-Waite-Smith tarot deck, but in her own time, she was renowned not just as an artist, but also as a poet, a storyteller, and a theater designer. She was born on February 16, 1878, in London, to wealthy American parents. They moved to Jamaica in 1888, where Pamela's nurse—a Black Jamaican woman—told her folktales. Pamela left at fifteen to study art at the Pratt Institute, only to return in 1896 to help care for her sick mother, who passed soon after. Following her mother's death, Pamela and her father moved to New York, where she began to pursue a career as a professional artist with help from well-connected family and friends, but in 1899, he unexpectedly passed, and Pamela returned to the city of her birth. Once she had settled in, Pamela began hosting a weekly gathering of artists and other bohemians.

In 1901, she met W. B. Yeats and joined his Temple of the Golden Dawn; it is through this group that she later met Arthur Waite. Her art became more mystical and symbolic as the decade progressed, and she continued to move in elite social circles. In 1907, Pamela wrote an article exhorting new artists to express their true selves instead of conforming to trends; she herself regularly rejected social norms in her art and in her personal life, in true Aquarian style!

Pamela finished the artwork for Arthur Waite's deck of tarot cards in 1909; he had felt that the tarot could be improved by adding symbolic illustrations to the pip cards. Waite referred to Pamela as "a most imaginative and abnormally psychic artist," though it remains unclear how much artistic direction he gave Pamela. Today, this deck is commonly known as the Rider-Waite tarot deck, after Waite and his publisher, obscuring Pamela's contribution.

During this decade, Pamela also often performed her Jamaican folktale retellings while brightly costumed and speaking in patois. Perhaps because of this affectation, there have been persistent rumors—beginning during her life—that Pamela was multiracial. They may have begun as a way to explain both her affinity for Jamaican folklore and her habit of defying expectations. However, no evidence has been found to support them; her ancestry is well documented, and she strongly resembles portraits of her close family members on both sides.

In 1914, Pamela stopped hosting her gatherings and faded from the public eye, and she was heavily in debt by the time she died in Bude in 1951. She was given a Roman Catholic funeral, as she had converted in 1911, but there was no money to pay for the transportation of her body to the nearest Catholic cemetery or for a headstone, so she was buried in an unmarked grave at St. Michael's Anglican Church in Bude. Her exact resting place is now unknown, due to burial records being destroyed in a fire; a demeaning end for such a bright Aquarian star.

Bibliography

+ Kaplan, Stuart R., with Mary K. Greer, Elizabeth Foley O'Connor, and Melinda Boyd Parsons. *Pamela Colman Smith: The Untold Story.* Stamford, CT: US Games Systems, 2018.
+ Norfleet, Phil. "Ancestry of Pamela Colman Smith." Biography of Pamela Colman Smith. Last modified March 30, 2011. https://pcs2051.tripod.com/ancestors.htm.

A Sampling of Aquarius Occultists

CORA ANN ANDERSON
one of the founders of the Feri Tradition
(January 26, 1915)

———————

EDMUND "EDDIE" BUCZYNSKI
founder of the Minoan Brotherhood
(January 28, 1947)

———————

PAULINE CAMPANELLI
renowned artist, witch, and occult author
(January 25, 1943)

———————

ROBERT COCHRANE
founder of the Clan of Tubal Cain Tradition
(January 26, 1931)

———————

PHYLLIS CUROTT
attorney, author, and Wiccan Priestess
(February 8, 1954)

———————

PATRICIA MONAGHAN
Goddess spirituality activist and author
(February 15, 1946)

———————

GABRIELLE ROTH
dancer, musician, and shaman
(February 4, 1941)

———————

THE SWAY OF YOUR MOON SIGN

Ivo Dominguez, Jr.

The Moon is the reservoir of your emotions, thoughts, and all your experiences. The Moon is your subconscious, your unconscious, and your instinctive response in the moment. The Moon is also the author, the narrator, and the musical score in the ongoing movie in your mind that summarizes and mythologizes your story. The Moon is like a scrying mirror, a sacred well, that gives answers to the question of the meaning of your life. The style and the perspective of your Moon sign shapes your story, a story that starts as a reflection of your Sun sign's impetus. The remembrance of your life events is a condensed subjective story, and it is your Moon sign that summarizes and categorizes the data stream of your life.

In witchcraft, the Moon is our connection and guide to the physical and energetic tides in nature, the astral plane, and other realities. The Moon in the heavens as it moves through signs and phases also pulls and pushes on your aura. The Moon in your birth chart reveals the intrinsic qualities and patterns in your aura, which affects the form your magick takes. Your Sun sign may be the source of your essence and power, but your Moon sign shows how you use that power in your magick. This chapter describes the twelve possible arrangements of Moon signs with an Aquarius Sun and what each combination yields.

Moon in Aries

You are courageous, clever, and often rebellious. You love to shake things up and change for the sake of change. Together these two signs increase your desire to be a unique individual, and fitting in is low on your list of priorities. You move fast and are an excellent problem-solver. Your thinking is solid and your insights are on point. However, you may create new problems along the way because in your haste, you may not listen closely enough to others. Once in motion, you can be a juggernaut. You are amiable, witty, and can be a lot of fun, which helps smooth over these incidents. Always remember to use your sense of humor. You need regular social interaction to keep balanced and on track in your life more than most Aquarians. You may desire to be a loner, but it rarely works. You are passionate but tend to express the cooler, gentler emotions less frequently.

You need to have several categories of friends so that you'll have a pool to draw on when you have a spontaneous urge to do something. You may be frustrated that others don't want to move at your pace or disagree with your opinions. The more you release your expectations about people, the closer you'll be to your friends and partners. They also need to be able to hold their own and say no and stand up for what they believe to gain your respect. You are devoted to friends and lovers who are always growing, and if they aren't, you lose interest. Your thoughts are fast, and you are very perceptive, but that speedy flow also makes it harder to retain orderly memories. Note-taking, calendars, and recordings are your friend. These two signs make you a visionary and a pathfinder, so you need work that engages these skills.

An Aries Moon, like all the fire element Moons, easily stretches forth to connect with the energy of other beings. The fiery qualities cleanse and protect your aura from picking up other people's emotional debris or being influenced by your environment. It is relatively easy for you to blend your energy with others and to separate cleanly. Your Aquarius Sun uses this rising's characteristics to extend the range and power of your spells and workings. This combination assists in raising and shaping power for yourself and others. You may have a gift for creating or destroying thoughtforms and clearing negative energy.

Moon in Taurus

Like all Aquarians you think things through, but with a Taurus Moon, your head may do all the processing, but your heart calls the shots. Your behavior is often seen as admirable, reasonable, and honorable. You prefer peace, but you are a reformer, and when needed, those Taurean horns come out. You tend to be more of a protector than a fighter and want to use your power for the benefit of others. Both Aquarius and Taurus are fixed signs, which makes you determined or stubborn depending on circumstances and perspectives. Your sense of purpose and confidence tend to make people follow your lead. You like your privacy and try to work without attracting too much public attention. Your sense of privacy is one of the reasons people come to you for your ear and support.

The Moon is said to be exalted in Taurus, which gives it greater power to add more poise and centeredness to your personality. It makes you more likely to achieve mundane goals as well as emotional ones. You are more sensual than most Aquarians. This leads to a love of food, the arts, and physical pleasures of every type. This could mean creating poetry, art, architecture, a garden, an annual event, or almost anything else that others can experience. You would be good at selling or teaching or anything where you are changing hearts and minds. If you find yourself slowing down or getting stuck in the same circumstances, spending time outdoors in nature is your best restorative. Another option is hosting a small social gathering or meal in your home.

A Taurus Moon, like all the earth element Moons, generates an aura that is magnetic and pulls energy inward. This Moon also makes it easier to create strong shields and wards. The auras of people with a Taurus Moon are excellent at holding or restoring a pattern or acting as a container or vessel in a working. You do well acting in the role of summoner or as a vessel to attract spirits to you; you are the destination rather than the traveler to their realms. You have an aptitude for communicating with the Fae, nature spirits, and elementals. Take care that you fully release those connections when you are done. You also have a knack for beacon magick to attract people or situations that you need and for spells that repel what you do not desire.

♊

Moon in Gemini

A double dose of air energy makes you a talker, a thinker, and a daydreamer. You are energetic, lively, and often your tongue can't keep in sync with your speeding mind. You communicate several ideas at once, which can come out as brilliant or confusing depending on the listener and your speed. You need more of a filter on what comes out of your mouth. A little self-censorship would probably serve you well. It is important to allocate your resources wisely because you love doing several things at once. You are brilliant, adaptable, and original, but time is a limited resource. You are enthusiastic at the beginning of things but tend to run out of steam. You like thrills and adrenaline, but those fuels burn fast. Work on recruiting people around you who like the details and can trudge through the slow parts.

Because you are so easygoing and gregarious, it can be hard to tell if you are flirting, being friendly, doing professional networking, and so on. You have many people in your life but few who are truly close. When you fall for someone, it is as sudden and bright as a flash of lightning. The hard work comes in making the transition from the brilliance of that flash to the softer radiance of lasting relationships. The people closest to you need to be adventurous, creative, and understanding of your changeable moods and interests. Developing the habit of caution and contemplation before jumping into action will benefit every part of your life. Travel, or even reading about travel, can relax or energize you as needed. Music and art, especially from cultures other than your own, are especially invigorating for you.

A Gemini Moon, like all the air Moons, makes it easier to engage in soul travel and psychism and gives the aura greater flexibility. When an air aura reaches out and touches something, it can quickly read and copy the patterns it finds. A Gemini Moon gives the capacity to quickly adapt and respond to changing energy conditions in working magick or using the psychic senses. A wind can pick up and carry dust and debris, and the same is true for an aura. If you need to cleanse your energy, become as still as you can, and the debris will simply fall out of your aura. You are good at writing invocations, spells, and rituals with a gift for deflecting or changing magick that has already been cast.

Moon in Cancer

This Moon makes you more emotional than most Aquarians. This can give you insight into other people and add more heart to the work you do in causes to improve the lot of humanity. You have a greater need for approval and connection with people, which can lead to insecurity but opens you to seek deeper connections with people. When you have the right mixture of Cancer heart and Aquarian mind, you are intuitive, influential, and admired. This combination also brings a desire to bring forward the best of the past as you create the future. Cancer loves the past and Aquarius longs for the future, which can produce great adaptability. Like most Aquarians, you like the unconventional, the eccentric, and bending the rules. Your Cancer Moon mellows this a bit so that your idealism is well tempered with compassion. At work or at home, it is important that you learn to release negative feelings about yourself or others. This combination tends to remember and replay difficult memories.

You love being around people, but until you know someone well, you do not open up or share anything of consequence. You can be so charming that people don't realize you've been keeping them at bay with pleasant, light, safe conversation. It's understandable because once trust is broken or you are hurt, it is hard for you to move on. Many people with this combination were very sensitive as children, so there tends to be a backlog of things to process. You have a substantial sense of personal pride and dignity that you guard. You are a protector, so if someone is harmed, you will do all you can to remedy the situation. Although philosophical about humanity like most Aquarians, you are drawn to seeing humanity as your extended family.

A Cancer Moon, like all the water Moons, gives the aura a magnetic pull that wants to merge with whatever is nearby. Imagine two drops of water growing closer until they barely touch and how they pull together to become one larger drop. The aura of a person with a Cancer Moon is more likely to absorb the patterns and energies it touches. This matters even when doing solo workings or divination. Spells, readings, or rituals can get stuck in your head like a song on repeat, so cleanse thoroughly. This combination usually comes with a gift for peacemaking, divination that applies to groups of people, past-life regression, and lunar magick.

Moon in Leo

You are called to leadership, to be at the center of things, and trendsetting more than most Aquarians. Be clear on what your role, image, and desired outcomes should be and you'll stay on track. You radiate self-assurance even when you are not sure of yourself. Your ideals are central to how you live your life. You aim for larger than life, and the story you tell can excite and enliven other people. You have a fascination with the big picture in life, so religion, spirituality, and the occult will always attract your interest. Both your Sun and Moon are in fixed signs, which gifts you with confidence and strength of character but may also make you prone to an excess of pride and inflexibility. When you focus on winning people over rather than arguing them into agreement, everyone wins.

This combination tends to be highly romantic and idealistic about people, and equally so toward the arts, media, or causes. There is a devotional undertone to almost everything in your life. Those who are close to you need to be able to reel you in when you are burning a bit too brightly. You don't know when to stop whether it is work or play. Your friends and loved ones need to be secure in their self-worth so that they can truly be your peers. You reinvent yourself so many times over the course of your life that you are not always sure of who you are in the moment. You do best with solid input from people who know you well. You have too many goals to accomplish well in a lifetime, and you want excellence. Actively ask the universe for clues and guidance rather than using trial and error and educated guesses on what to pursue and what to shelve.

A Leo Moon, like all the fire element Moons, easily stretches forth to connect with the energy of other beings, though a little bit less than Aries and Sagittarius. The fiery qualities act to cleanse and protect your aura from picking up other people's emotional debris or being influenced by your environment. It is relatively easy for you to blend your energy with others and to separate cleanly. The Leo Moon also makes it easier for you to find your center and stay centered. Your magick is well suited to helping others transform, healing, love, and glamour. You also can act as a catalyst that awakens magick in the people around you when you reach out your energy.

Moon in Virgo

This Moon adds Virgo's sharp analytical powers to Aquarius's airy mentality. The detail focus of Virgo with the Aquarian aptitude for understanding systems is hard to beat. You are an independent, clear-thinking visionary with a sense of duty, which is a rare set of qualities. You are also a close observer of the human condition, nature, and society. You are highly principled and like to follow your core beliefs in both the letter and the spirit of the law. The downside to this combination is that it is vulnerable to anxiety and harsh self-criticism. You know how to select and put people and resources together to create effective teams and projects. Your expectations tend to be just outside the range of the probable. Moreover, you can't control everything, no matter how hard you try. Work on letting go of frustration when your standards are not met.

You seem more conservative than most Aquarians, but in truth you are just as eccentric but try to repurpose the conventional tools that are easily available. You like to work unnoticed in the background until you are ready to share something. You are often perceived to be cool and detached, so it is harder for people to guess when you want support or reassurance. You have an air of self-sufficiency, which is mostly accurate, but your need for connection and human warmth is more than you let yourself realize. You offer help to many other people; let them balance the equation by offering you assistance. Compassion for yourself is necessary for your physical and mental health. You have plans and desires but are modest in your approach and tend not to be motivated by glory. Make sure that the look and feel of your home and work environment is as streamlined and as soothing as possible. This has an impact on your health and happiness. Paradoxically, in addition to time in solitude, debating with a friend and testing ideas is also very relaxing for you.

A Virgo Moon, like all the earth element Moons, generates an aura that is magnetic and pulls energy inward. This Moon also makes it easier to create strong thoughtforms and energy constructs. You have strong shields, but if breached, your shields tend to hang on to the pattern of injury; get some healing help, or the recovery may take longer than it should. Spells and workings related to seeking truth, cleansing, bindings, and agreements are assisted by this Moon. You can develop a gift for financial and business magick.

♎

Moon in Libra

The cardinal air of Libra enlivens the fixed air of Aquarius. It brings forth kindness, an easy wit, and charisma. You are a social creature, and it doesn't matter if you are an extrovert, an introvert, or an ambivert, you need time with people to do your work in the world and to stay mentally balanced. You stand out in a crowd, and even when you are trying to fit in, something quirky will pop out. Whatever tasks you take on at home or in the workplace, you need to work fast and put your best effort at the start. Your usual pattern is a big burst of energy at the start of things and then a drop as your initial enthusiasm wanes. Plan for this by learning to reframe things to re-create the sense of newness that brings back your energy and interest.

Although you are caring and accommodating to your friends and partners, they may feel that after a time you are drifting away. Express your feelings regularly so that the people in your life don't rely on guesswork to know their standing. Another option is to arrange events, experiences, or outings to enjoy together. In general, you do better with friends and partners who want you but don't need you. Make more time in your life for your spiritual and magickal endeavors, as these activities truly feed your soul. You are tolerant and open-minded about most things so long as your happiness, and that of your beloveds, is not at risk. Pick which battles you'll take on and which are a waste of your well-chosen words. You are inherently a member of many communities because you are a complex blend of identities. This can be a great benefit to you if used with awareness and finesse.

A Libra Moon, like all the air Moons, makes it easier to engage in soul travel and psychism and gives the aura greater flexibility. When you are working well with your Libra Moon, you can make yourself a neutral and clear channel for information from spirits and other entities. You are also able to tune in to unspoken requests when doing divinatory work. This Moon also helps you do work for creating art, making music, healing hearts, and encouraging personal development. Venus is Libra's ruling planet, so you also have a gift for the magick of love, beauty, self-worth, and the release of old sorrows.

Moon in Scorpio

A Scorpio Moon makes the classic traits of Aquarius more intense and prominent. You also have more emotions, passions, drives, and internal storms than most Aquarians. Scorpio Moon gives you more determination, and that means when you commit, you are all in. You would make a great researcher, investigator, or anything that requires long-term drive and determination. You have little time for social conventions and your personality will produce a wide range of reactions in other people. And these reactions and opinions will mostly cluster to the extremes; you aren't a middle ground kind of person. Your opinions, on just about everything, also tend to be strong and distinctive. This can put you at odds with rules and authority. Learning to moderate this tendency is crucial to the best use of your time and energy.

When you take an interest in someone, you can be remarkably intense. Try to ramp up slowly so you don't scare people off. This Sun and Moon blend also makes it easier to notice the darkness and turbulence within yourself and in the world. You can swing between being overly proud and your own worst critic. The middle between these two is the personal truth you are looking for. Learning to laugh at your own foibles is the first and most important step. The more you embrace your whole self, the easier it will be to deal with the world. Scorpio Moon gives you an air of mystery and sensual magnetism. You do love your secrets, and other people love to tell you their secrets; this is a sacred trust. How well you keep them is how well you will feel about yourself. You are not immune to envy or jealousy, and both are dangerous for you.

A Scorpio Moon, like all the water Moons, gives the aura a magnetic pull that wants to merge with whatever is nearby. You easily absorb information about other people, spirits, places, and so on. Your path for purification is to feel things fully so you can fully release them. Your words or thoughts can turn into magick when you are emotional, so be careful. You have a gift for sigil work, creating servitors and thoughtforms, designing altars and shrines, and writing and performing incantations and invocations. Mediumship is an option for you, but you need to have spirit guides or human warders while you do the work so that you feel comfortable enough to go deeper.

Moon in Sagittarius

This Moon makes you more inspirational, buoyant, and the kind of forward thinker who finds themselves in leadership roles. You tend toward optimism and seeing the glass as half full. And as an Aquarian, you are dreaming up the ways to fill the glass as well. However, when things are truly a mess, you will tell your story as if it were an epic saga where good triumphs in the end. You are good at looking at all the available information and making predictions that border on the prophetic when it involves the big picture. This combination makes the desire to turn the *ideal* into the *real* the core of your being. If you feel that your freedom to act is impinged upon, you can become short-fused and antagonistic.

Your exuberance and inspiration often put you in the spotlight. Your reputation is often shaped by what you've said in a moment of passion. In your excitement to get things moving you will often be tactless. When it doesn't work out, remember that you have humor and a silver-tongue on your side. In the end, even your adversaries are likely to admit you have admirable traits. You try to be generous whenever you can. You are affectionate, playful, and often romantic, but you need lots of space and freedom in your relationships. You also have a bit of a competitive streak in your temperament. You enjoy traveling, and going on a trip with someone is a good way to gauge long-term compatibility.

The auras of people with Sagittarius Moon are the most adaptable of the fire Moons. Your energy can reach far and change its shape easily. You are particularly good at affecting other people's energy or the energy of a place. Like the other fire Moons, your aura is good at cleansing itself, but it is not automatic and requires your conscious choice. This is because the mutable fire of Sagittarius is change-able and can go from a small ember to a pillar of fire that reaches the sky. You may have a favorite type or style of witchcraft or magick, but you are a general-ist at heart. You can fit into a wide range of tradi-tions and rituals so well that you may be mistaken for being a member when you are a guest. You have a gift for magick to remove roadblocks, release ties to people, increase psychism, and divine for large-scale questions.

Moon in Capricorn

The earthiness of Capricorn and Saturn as its ruler gives you much appreciated grounding and practicality. You are an Aquarian who wants to make your mark on the world, and you have no problem rolling up your sleeves and getting down to work. You have as strong a love of tradition as you do of forging a new path forward. You will succeed in almost anything you choose because you are tenacious and stay restless until you accomplish what you set out to do. You do have to watch your level of frustration when things move too slowly because if not managed properly it turns into irritability. Be careful not to overcontrol your emotions or you may fuel stress-related illness. You need to feel financially safe to avoid distress; this is one of your strongest motivators.

Your communication skills and sense of purpose make you influential. You didn't have the easiest of childhoods, but it gave you strength and powerful lessons. That is all the motivation you need to do what you can to make things better. Your principles and the people you trust will keep you grounded and connected to your hopes. Learning to accept other people's frailties can be challenging with this Sun and Moon combination. There is a tendency to expect too much of yourself, and when events bring about a failure, you think too little of yourself. Take stock of the facts and assess who you are and who you want to be so you can plan but not judge. You like to think that you're a loner, but you are not. Don't be stubborn and allow yourself to be open to your feelings. In love and friendship, you are caring, reliable, and encouraging. Just make sure your needs get met too.

A Capricorn Moon, like all the earth element Moons, generates an aura that is magnetic and pulls energy inward. What you draw to yourself tends to stick and solidify, so be wary, especially when doing healing work or cleansings. Call on the air of your Aquarius Sun to keep things fresh. The magick of a Capricorn Moon is excellent at imposing a pattern or creating a container in a working. Your spells and workings tend to be durable and long lasting. You have a talent for jar spells and magick pouches, working with crystals, business spells, and bindings. Oracular and trance work is something you may want to try.

~~~

Moon in Aquarius

With both your Sun and Moon in Aquarius signs, you are avant-garde, experimental, and like to live in the moment. You are highly original and resilient against attempts to make you fall in line. You tend to be bold, inventive, and playful in most arenas of your life. Your impulsive and spontaneous nature excites and sometimes frightens your friends. You are always searching for novelty and the next new experience or idea. Staying focused and on track is not one of your natural gifts. The sooner in life you learn methods to manage or trick yourself into following through on your ideas, the happier you will be. Try to choose careers or courses of study that have lots of change and novelty and you'll do better. You tend to experience routines and strict schedules as torment. Also, you are ahead of your time, so keep records so that you can bring those ideas to light when the time is right.

This combination lets you see many different angles and perspectives at once, so you will often notice details and trends others miss. Make use of the opportunities that information creates. Knowing is good but doing is better. You are a better analyst than you are a manager, so find other people who can implement your ideas. You spend so much time observing others and your surroundings that you may get lost in your thoughts. Friends who make you come out of your head and into life are essential. Although you are tolerant and broad-minded, you tend to only become close to people who share a good portion of your core values. Take your time and learn from each relationship as you go. You have a gift for creating graceful cooperation between people, in an organization, working on a project, in a social group, and so on. This will be one of the keys to your success.

Like all the air Moons, the Aquarius Moon encourages a highly mobile and flexible aura. You have an air Moon, so grounding is important, but focusing on your core and center is more important. From that center, you can strengthen and stabilize your power. People with an Aquarius Moon are good at shaping and holding a specific thoughtform or energy pattern and transferring it to other people or into objects. You have skill in divination for groups, whether that be covens, businesses, nations, or circumstances that affect many. There is also a gift for enchanting objects and perhaps for bringing out latent talents in others.

Moon in Pisces

You are more feeling and altruistic than most other Aquarians. The humanitarian qualities of Aquarius take on a distinctly personal touch with this Moon. You have strong intuition and psychism when you let your barriers soften. The downside is that it is easier for you to get ungrounded and drift off. You are good at spotting deception, understanding undercurrents in events around you, but with a weakness. You can be fooled by those who offer you friendship or love. Although it is generally admirable to look for the best in people, it is also wise to use your intellect and intuition to see the whole truth. You have a sparkling personality that exudes a basically hopeful view on life. You are a weird magnet, and you would not want it any other way. You look for and attract the unusual and the extraordinary. Do be careful lest your imagination lead to fantasies that keep you from living in the here and now.

Your imagination and creativity will open the way for many career options. This doesn't necessarily mean you will be in the arts, but it does mean that your originality will be the key to success. For example, you can always come up with several ways to describe or explain something, which is useful in teaching, negotiating, and so on. You also have a strong intellect to ground your insight and creativity with facts and plausible theories. You give off a welcoming air and have an endearing sense of humor and whimsy that will help both your work and your home life. With your words and your actions, you demonstrate your belief that all people are worthy of their rights and a place at the table.

With a Pisces Moon, the emphasis should be on learning to feel and control the rhythm of your energetic motion in your aura. Pisces Moon is the most likely to pick up and hang on to unwanted emotions or energies. Rippling your energy and bouncing things off the outer layers of your aura is a good defense. Be careful, develop good shielding practices, and make cleansing yourself and your home a regular practice. Practices that involve going into trance come easily for you, but make sure you have a helper. Your storytelling is a form of magick as well and you may wish to write visualizations and pathworkings. Dreamwork is also one of your strong suits. You would be a good medium, but get trained for the sake of safety.

TAROT
CORRESPONDENCES
Ivo Dominguez, Jr.

You can use the tarot cards in your work as an Aquarius witch for more than divination. They can be used as focal points in meditations and trance to connect with the power of your sign or element or to understand it more fully. They are great on your altar as an anchor for the powers you are calling. You can use the Minor Arcana cards to tap into Venus, Mercury, or Moon in Aquarius energy even when they are in other signs in the heavens. If you take a picture of a card, shrink the image and print it out; you can fold it up and place it in spell bags or jars as an ingredient.

Aquarius Major Arcana

The Star

All the Air Signs

The Ace of Swords

Aquarius Minor Arcana

5 of Swords	Venus in Aquarius
6 of Swords	Mercury in Aquarius
7 of Swords	Moon in Aquarius

• MY MOST AQUARIUS WITCH MOMENT •

Mickie Mueller

I've had a lot of Aquarius witch moments, and I want to share one that was pivotal for me. This is a story about how a spur-of-the-moment innovative spell, an exploding bridge, and getting out of my comfort zone, led to me creating an online witchcraft community!

It was early April of 2019. My husband and I were on our way home from visiting family. I was driving our car across the Missouri River on a newly constructed modern streamlined bridge that was right next to the decommissioned and more charming historic Highway 47 bridge in Washington, MO. We were talking about what was going to happen to the old bridge when Dan's keen eye noticed there were explosive charges attached all along the length of the old landmark. Upon arriving home, he did a little digging and found the day and time they planned to demolish the bridge. Since it's only forty minutes away from where we live, he suggested that it would be a really cool thing to go watch. Dan and I both appreciate history and we have driven over that old bridge probably over a hundred times. It was built in the 1930s and had seen better days as it had become notoriously scary for commuters to use. That old bridge was useful in its time but was now obsolete, no longer safe, and no longer needed. Although it had charm and memories, it was time to say goodbye.

We showed up at the park by the riverfront and found a place to sit in the grass as people began to fill the park around us. This was a moment in time that spoke to this Aquarius witch; I thought of Janus, the Roman god of time, gates, and transitions, who looks simultaneously to the past and the future. We were looking backward in time at the endearing old bridge with fond memories and forward to the new safer one that would be part of all our future journeys. As more people arrived at the park, the place began to erupt into a carnival atmosphere. My witch's heart was buzzing with the excitement in the air, some people were snacking, listening to music; there were news helicopters overhead. I could hear people around us sharing memories with each other about this landmark. This was an important moment in time for this city and we were all here to witness the official changing of the guard of our passage across this stretch of beautiful

Missouri River. I decided in that moment to post about it on social media, just a photo and a few words about what we were up to that morning to share the moment with anyone who might be interested. As Aquarian witches, our independent nature is often at odds with our need to belong to part of a community. Sure, we can show up at a gathering and choose to linger as an outsider observing and analyzing, or we can turn on the charm as the weird and eccentric life of the party. At this point in my life, I had been spending too much time firmly in independence mode, on the edges of the party. Something in that day pushed me out of my comfort zone.

My social media friends began to excitedly comment on my post; several people were suggesting that I should go live so they could watch it happen too. I didn't even know how to do that, but I decided I would try. I had invited them to the party, so now I had to deliver! But that wasn't enough. In addition, that very moment in that big crowd of people, I also decided that I could turn this moment into a spell! Innovation is my favorite flavor of Aquarian magick, and my mind loves to play with new ways of doing things and new ways to think about magick. I not only figured out how to broadcast a live video on my page, which I had never done before, but I also found the little box to add a description before going live. I informed my viewers in the description that we were watching them blow up a grand old bridge over the Missouri River in real time and to feel free to visualize something that used to be necessary in their life but now has no purpose and imagine it's on the bridge. I suggested releasing emotional baggage such as unfounded fears or a negative self-image. Sometimes we create these mindsets as coping mechanisms to get us through a hard time, but it's healthy to let them go when we no longer need them. Opportunities for magick are everywhere if you look with the eyes of an Aquarian witch. We would watch together as what we needed to release would crumble into the flowing river to be cleansed away! What did I envision on that bridge? I'll tell you. Some of my fears surrounding being heard and taking up space!

Next thing I knew I was doing my best newscaster routine live for everyone to see as I explained what was happening, tidbits we had heard about the demolition crew, and gave the general play-by-play of the event. Even Dan got caught up in the moment and comically quipped off camera, "I just wanted to come here for a nice quiet day at the park and all these people showed up!" We were really having fun with it! And then in a moment, through my shaky and completely unprofessional camerawork, we watched that bridge drop in a flash! How many of my viewers' doubts and fears were on that bridge when it collapsed into the swirling depths of the Missouri River? I can't say, but I hope it was as powerful for them as it was for me. The hair on my arms still stands up when I think of it. The next moment the deep resonating boom hit us so forcefully that I could feel it in my whole body. The crowd erupted in wild cheering! This was the moment we had all waited for! I ended the live video, but damn, I was hooked.

I said to myself, "That was really fun, why had I been so nervous to be on camera anyway?" I had been called a big ham as a kid. My acting had won multiple awards and even a role in a college production when I was in high school. I used to be an MC at a rock and metal club in the 1990s. I realized that one difficult life experience after the other in my later adulthood had chipped away my confidence, leaving me feeling small, and I had put up a wall around myself. I hadn't been true to that outgoing part of my Aquarian nature for a while until that morning in the park by the river. Clearly that last-minute spell I wove in a crowd full of people watching a bridge explode had shifted something within me.

Over the next couple of weeks, I dove deep and directed my Aquarian witch hyperfocus toward teaching myself how to make and edit videos and create a YouTube channel. I used what I had: my phone, one slightly used tripod ring light held together with gaffer tape, and sheer nerve. On May 1, less than a month after the bridge explosion spell, I launched my YouTube channel with a Beltane spell I had crafted that used a bit of old folklore about washing your face in the dew on Beltane morning. My channel grew quickly, and soon I was getting to know some of the other witches I had admired and enjoyed watching on the platform. I was enjoying all the comments and had fun expanding on the video content while answering my viewers' questions about the spells and magickal techniques I shared in the videos. My channel was turning into a community, and I was enjoying learning from my commentors as much as I enjoyed teaching them.

The more videos I made, the more I began to tease apart the different aspects of my own witchcraft practice. In order to explain something step-by-step in a video, you really have to analyze what you do. As I had already been a practicing witch for more than twenty years at the time, much of what I did on my own just came naturally, like muscle memory. Breaking it down for others helped me look at why I work the way I do and even inspired new ways of doing things. Something else that has inspired me was realizing that my viewers live all over the world and not all of them have access to the same materials or tools. Because of this, I've focused my videos on something I've done my whole life: making do with what I have on hand. I try to remind the people I teach that it's not the things, ingredients, or tools that hold the real magick, but the witch themselves. That's why I tell people to "be your magick." That was what I did in that spell in the park, I just listened to what my Aquarian witch heart said. I looked around at what I had in the moment, innovated, and created a shift.

YOUR RISING SIGN'S INFLUENCE

Ivo Dominguez, Jr.

The rising sign, also known as the ascendant, is the sign that was rising on the eastern horizon at the time and place of your birth. In the birth chart, it is on the left side on the horizontal line that divides the upper and lower halves of the chart. Your rising sign is also the cusp of your first house. It is often said that the rising sign is the mask you wear to the world, but it is much more than that. It is also the portal through which you experience the world. The sign of your ascendant colors and filters those experiences. Additionally, when people first meet you, they meet your rising sign. This means they interact with you based on their perception of that sign rather than your Sun sign. This in turn has an impact on you and how you view yourself. As they get to know you over time, they'll meet you as your Sun sign. Your ascendant is like the colorful clouds that hide the Sun at dawn, and as the Sun continues to rise, it is revealed.

The rising sign also has an influence on your physical appearance as well as your style of dress. To some degree, your voice, mannerisms, facial expressions, stance, and gait are also swayed by the sign of your ascendant. The building blocks of your public persona come from your rising sign. How you arrange those building blocks is guided by your Sun sign, but your Sun sign must work with what it has been given. For witches, the rising sign shows some of the qualities and foundations for the magickal personality you can construct. The magickal personality is much more than simply shifting into the right headspace, collecting ritual gear, lighting candles, and so on. The magickal persona is a construct that is developed through your magickal and spiritual practices to serve as an interface between different parts of the self. The magickal persona, also known as the magickal personality, can also act as a container or boundary so that the mundane and the magickal parts of a person's life can each have its own space. Your rising also gives clues about which magickal techniques will come naturally to you.

This chapter describes the twelve possible arrangements of rising signs with an Aquarius Sun and what each combination produces. There are 144 possible kinds of Aquarians when you take into consideration the Moon signs and rising signs. You may wish to reread the chapter on your Moon sign after reading about your rising sign so you can better understand these influences when they are merged.

Aries Rising

This rising makes you a warrior for any and all causes, big and small, that strike your fancy. This mixture of vision, courage, and vitality prods you to act. Your exterior is very outgoing and bold, but your inner self is always wondering how you get yourself into such complicated situations. You are a bit reckless and benefit from slowing down and taking stock of the details. Most people with this combination benefit from physical practices that are well structured and become a routine. It doesn't matter whether it is yoga, tai chi, dance—so long as you do it. This consumes excess energy so you can concentrate and reduces your stress.

Aries's cardinal fire mixed with Aquarius's fixed air definitely makes you spicy, salty, and sweet, but almost never sour. You alternate between zany, intellectual, rebellious, and zealous at the drop of a hat. Be advised that not everyone understands your verbal sparring and physical humor are meant as harmless fun or sometimes flirting. This combo loves a good debate, and you are competitive and relentless. You would make a good lawyer, advocate, community organizer, and so on. You are more aggressive than most other Aquarians but most of the energy is directed toward your causes and concerns. When you fall into a rugged individualist or a "me against the world" mindset, trouble follows. You are also quicker to jump into relationships, contracts, and so on.

An Aries rising means that when you reach out to draw in power, both air and fire will answer easily. If you need other types of energy, you need to reach farther, focus harder, and be more specific in your request. This combination often attracts the attention of the spirits, Fae, nature spirits, and other beings, so be mindful of what you say aloud. You excel at spells for political magick, confidence, or removing obstacles. These can be cast for yourself or others.

Taurus Rising

Taurus gives you the grounding of Earth with a Venus rulership that lets you enjoy life. This rising makes you more likely to slow down enough to smell the roses and enjoy all the sensual delights of life. You love peace and mutual respect and strive to bring that into the world. You don't like arguments or conflict and if there is too much noise and emotional turmoil, you become distracted or obstinate. You have an inner tension between the desire for home and comfort and the desire to make the world more livable for others. You also yearn for tradition and want to break free from traditions. You understand people in a way that would make you a good entrepreneur or manager. You also have charisma and a magnetic pull on people.

A Taurus rising encourages you to be trustworthy, practical, circumspect, and frugal. This combination asks your Aquarius energy to be practical and down to earth. If you begin to slow down and are less productive, it is a sign you are not being fair to yourself and are running low on the juice of life. Rising signs change how you perceive things, and, combined with your Aquarius Sun, this blend allows you to see the way through the twists and turns of the labyrinth of society and diplomacy.

Taurus rising gives more strength in your aura and the capacity to maintain a more solid shape to your energy. This gives you stronger shields and allows you to create thoughtforms and spells that are longer lasting. This combination also makes you a better channel for other people's energy in group work because you can tolerate larger volumes of different types of energies. You can act as an amplifier to boost individuals or small groups to increase their inherent magickal or psychic abilities. Herbalism and plant magick would serve you well.

♊
Gemini Rising

A Gemini rising makes you even more of a talker and a thinker than most Aquarians. You don't even need to turn on the charm to be noticed. You often get your way through humor or gentle persuasion. You are always looking for new experiences, fresh conversation, new music, and styles that express your mood. You move easily between different age-groups, backgrounds, cultures, and so on. Learn to breathe deep and listen more than you speak. You have a considerable amount of raw talent for a variety of activities, but you often lose interest or lack the follow-through that leads to success. Develop systems to keep track of your important projects and recruit people to help you do your best.

Your friends and partners need to share your love of quickly changing activities. Friendship is also central to your romantic relationships. You tend to love complexity and that also affects your relationships. You love to communicate so make sure you talk with your friends and partners about expectations, agreements, and reciprocity. Your family of choice is very important to you. Your nervous system runs fast and tends to overheat. Find several relaxation or meditation practices that work for you so you can alternate between them. If you stick to only one, it is likely you'll bore of it and stop doing it.

This rising helps your energy and aura stretch farther and adapt to whatever it touches. This combination can lend itself to clairsentience, simply having information drop into your mind. You can pick up too much information and it can be overwhelming. Learn to narrow down and control your awareness of other people's thoughts and feelings. With work, you have a gift for understanding and healing injuries to the aura, the subtle bodies. You have an energy that can help or hinder technology and can impact the digital realm.

Cancer Rising

The emotional intuition of this rising combined with your intellectual Aquarius Sun gives you predictive insights into current and future trends. This sensitivity can be brought to bear in work as a teacher, counselor, translator, negotiator, and so on. There are many other ways you can use this skill. Balancing head and heart is important for everyone, but it is essential for you since your rising is so different from your Sun sign. The ideas you share may often be unexpected and thought-provoking. Try to remain neutral and don't jump to conclusions about how others feel about you. More often than not, they are processing your words rather than judging you.

Cancer rising gives you a love of the past and history and a touch of sentimentality. There is also a pull to be more nurturing and preserve living beings and material goods that have emotional value and memories attached to them. You tend to be drawn more to the generations before or after yours. At the same time you also have a drive to look to the future and create new ways to create comfort and security. The people close to you should be orderly, calm, and well grounded. It takes a bit to get you into a relationship, but once there, you are very giving and emotionally present. Your great gift is sensitivity, but you need safe and quiet places for rest and refuge. Music is one of the best restoratives for you.

Cancer rising grants the power to use your emotions, or the emotional energy of others, to power your witchcraft. Though you can draw on a wide range of energies to fuel your magick, raising power through emotion is the simplest method. This rising produces ease and power in Moon magick of any sort. You are also good at charging oils, waters, and other liquids. You may have a calling for creating altars, spiritual art, and house blessings.

Leo Rising

This combination has warmth and enthusiasm blended with a sharp intellect. Leo rising gives you a unique leadership style that is best suited to offering guidance and inspiration, but not the details of the daily grind. You have more stamina and determination than most Aquarians. This rising gives a great deal of self-confidence, however the downside is that, when thwarted, Leo rising mixed with those Aquarian winds can get very stormy. You regret your outbursts almost immediately even though you still feel that you were correct. You are one of the most companionable types of Aquarius. You also know how to either fit in or shock whatever group you are with. You understand styles and trends and choose to follow them, create new ones, or defy them as you wish.

This blend loves the good things in life, so don't forget to attend to your career needs. You are good at guiding people to do better, and this is best done by leading by example. If you preach or speak as an authority, you may push away the people you wish to influence. Showing is better than telling. You are fearless in most situations, except when you find out that you made an error or had the wrong information. Drink plenty of water every day because this air and fire combo needs a large amount of water to cool and cleanse you.

Leo rising means that when you reach out to draw in power, fire will answer first. If you need other types of energy, you need to reach farther, focus harder, and be more specific in your request. Your aura and energy are brighter and steadier than most people's, so you attract the attention of spirits, deities, and so on. Your Sun and rising give you an aptitude for energy healing, oracular work, and ritual theater. You also can control the emotional and spiritual atmosphere of a room with ease.

Virgo Rising

This rising increases your desire to find meaning in life and to understand its mysteries. You have a strong calling to be of service, to work for a healthier world. In your eagerness, you may neglect getting enough rest and recreation. You are a stickler for details, which can serve you well or drive you to distraction. You are prone to wanting perfection in all things and may expect too much of yourself and others. Don't turn your friends or coworkers into improvement projects, as nobody will be happy. You derive satisfaction from identifying and solving problems. You have a fervent wish for everyone in the world to be freer.

This rising often suggests deeply ingrained habits, set patterns of behavior, and strong preferences for how things are arranged in your home and workplace. These structures help you feel more at ease. This seems contradictory with the Aquarian desire to make everything new and different, but the more you change things, the greater the need for some special things that stay stable. This can sometimes incite conflict with peers, friends, or partners. If you explain why certain things matter to you, there will be fewer irritations. Both your Sun and rising have a propensity for worrying, so managing stress and minding your nutrition is essential.

This blend makes it easier to work with divinities who are connected to the element of air, wisdom, civilization, and stewardship. You are good at spells for creating peace, serenity, and clarity of mind. You are a good diagnostician who can figure out what is wrong with a ritual, what is preventing a healthy flow of energy in a person or home, and so on. Be careful when you entwine your energy with someone else because you can pick up and retain their patterns and issues. Always cleanse your energy after doing solo or collective work.

♎

Libra Rising

You are more diplomatic and socially adept than most Aquarians. You are seen as likeable and friendly and give a great impression in most settings. Use your power to fascinate others with kindness. You know how to be just outrageous or flamboyant enough to make a splash, to rock the boat, but without capsizing it. If you are honest with yourself, you prefer to be a rolling stone than a cornerstone. People may experience you as unreliable unless you make it clear from the start that you are not making a commitment. You get things started, and when things seem stable enough, you want to move on. You need to have a variety of experiences and a change of scenery regularly.

You are good at reading people's intentions and truthfulness. Your voice can be commanding while remaining gentle. You may have a gift for working with animals, children, or people in distress. You have a great deal of creativity and resourcefulness so find careers that let you use those gifts. Learn to say no when you don't want to take on a task or your reputation will suffer. Encourage people to solve their own problems by empowering and mentoring them. Your work is also about changing the world, not just dispensing Band-Aids. Be mindful of endocrine or immune issues as balance in your body is the key to health. Be especially careful with the impact alcohol or other substances can have on you.

When you expand your aura, your personal energy can settle down an unruly or unwholesome atmosphere or calm down irritated spirits. Magick related to bringing peace or justice is favored by this combination. Rituals or spells to mend friendships and relationships or improve communication are favored. This combination also works well in creating jewelry, amulets, charms, working altars, or other physical instances of beauty and magick.

Scorpio Rising

You are openly passionate and enthusiastic and lack the aloofness or detachment that Aquarians often have. You are not darker than most Aquarians, you are just more aware of your dark side. You scrutinize, you dig, and you dispel illusions with your piercing intellect. Self-knowledge is your holy grail. Your thought process is complicated, layered, and woven through with many strands of emotion. Though you are creative, you tend more toward investigation, research, or specialties that make the most of your probing mind. When given a choice, you will pick an unconventional approach or create a new one. You tend to cycle through periods of intense activity followed by retreats into peace and solitude.

This rising is cautious about sharing their deep self, so humor, snark, and hot takes will be used to hold others at arm's length. That said, you easily jump into the role of helper, mentor, or protector when you see a person in need. You have deep insights into what people need. You are often more forgiving of other people's mistakes than your own. You need privacy and security to truly open up and reveal yourself to others. The people closest to you must be able to match your need for deep intimacy and adventure, an uncommon combination.

Scorpio rising makes your energy capable of pushing through most energetic barriers. You can dissolve illusion or bring down wards or shields and see through to the truth. You may have an aptitude for breaking bindings and lifting oppressive spiritual atmospheres. It is important that you do regular cleansing work for yourself. You are likely to end up doing messy work and you do not have a nonstick aura. You are a natural in rituals or workings for long-term divination, healing, or revealing secrets. Be cautious when making pledges, oaths, or promises in rituals.

Sagittarius Rising

This rising brings the fire of enthusiasm and optimism to your Aquarian thoughts. When fire and air mix well, you rocket toward your goals. When things go awry, you shake it off and try again, because a Sagittarius rising gives resilience. You value direct speech, which means your bluntness can get you into predicaments, but you often smooth things over with your positive intentions. You are often surprised by the effect that your statements have on people. You are constantly looking to improve yourself, but the first thing you need is more follow-through and sticking to your plans. You are more successful when you are doing so for a cause or another person.

You are more animated and outgoing than most Aquarians. You enjoy a wide range of social settings and having a diverse mix of people in your life. Your personal style and taste is often a mixture of many influences. You are very independent and follow your own conscience and inner guidance. Travel, sightseeing, and exploring new locations is important for your mental well-being. Physical activity, whether it is sports, dancing, hiking, or whatever you can manage, is essential for your health. This combo lets you appreciate and enjoy food and drink, sometimes to excess.

Sagittarius rising adds mutable fire to your fixed air so your aura changes shape at will and maintains patterns. Talent in the use of candles, wands, or crystals is favored by this combination. This is because you can push your energy and intentions into objects with ease. You have a talent for rituals and spells that call forth hope, enthusiasm, and abundance. You attract the attention of spirits and divine beings easily. You can be a voice for them if you wish. This combination gives access to lots of energy, but you can fry yourself with the intensity of the current. Make it your practice to stop and cool off and then start again.

Capricorn Rising

You give the impression of being more conservative and reserved than you really are. Since you are goal oriented, remind yourself that you can't do better unless you see your own progress and potential. A good amount of your self-esteem is tied to your work in the world. When you can harmonize the idealism of Aquarius with the practicality of Capricorn, you go far. Difficulties arise when the balance tips and you are too sure of your plans without the work to back them up. You are likely to choose long hours and hard work because you need to feel that you are not wasting your time.

You are a strong advocate, supporter, and sometimes defender of the people in your life. You have forceful needs and expectations in all your relationships, so you need people who can hold their own. You also do best with people who value stability and loyalty. You are very aware of human fragilities in yourself and in others, so it is important to learn how to manage your expectations for perfect behavior.

People may have trouble reading your emotions or intentions because Capricorn rising can hide them. Make it a practice to unambiguously reveal what needs to be shared and understood. Also pay more attention to your feelings about people.

Capricorn rising creates an aura and energy field that are slow to come up to speed but have amazing momentum once fully activated. Make it your habit to do some sort of energy work or meditative warm-up before engaging in witchcraft. Mandalas, mudras, and motion in general work well for you. Try working with chants, affirmations, and spoken spells. Your rituals and spells benefit from having a structure and a plan of action. Spells for persuasion, clear thinking, attracting resources, and business ventures are favored.

Aquarius Rising

This rising brings a second dose of Aquarian energy, which puts an emphasis on thought, communication, and breaking the rules. You buzz with an energy that others notice. For the most part, you are humanitarian and have a dozen plans, perspectives, and ideologies to make the world better. You like collective work and being on a team in theory, but you can find it hard to compromise. You don't wait for permission or approval to move forward. If you want to make your ideas real, you must meet reality in the middle. Find ways to make your ideas more practical. Your offbeat humor and eccentric views will help you find a way. You can't do all that you want without the cooperation of others, so make that a part of your planning process.

Caring about people arises from a mental and rational connection first that may, with time, become an emotional connection as well. You are not romantic in the normal sense of the word, but you do form strong bonds with people. You are passionate but rarely emotionally needy. Those close to you need to be equally innovative, freedom loving, and big-hearted. Stability is not your forte, so it would not hurt to keep people in your life who are grounded and established. Your nervous system is high-strung and needs no additional strains upon it, so be kind to yourself and get some rest.

Aquarius rising helps make it easier for you to consciously change the shape and density of your aura. This makes you a generalist who can adapt to many styles and forms of magick. Witchcraft focused on calling inspiration, creating community, and personal transformation are supported by this combination. Aquarius rising is gifted at turning ideas into reality. Mind magick, psychism, weather magick, and energy work are good options for you. Working with colors and scents helps your workings.

Pisces Rising

This rising brings in more mutability, flowing emotions, and psychic perceptions to complement Aquarius. Most of the time, you are sensitive, tender, caring, and aware of others' needs. You come across as a gentler and considerate Aquarian. Many people hold you in high regard, and you need to let them tell you how they see you. You are shyer and more modest than other Aquarians. This rising wants to avoid conflict and arguments, but your Aquarian ideals will eventually draw you into the fray. Your Sun lets you understand the plight of the world and your rising lets you feel it. Don't let melancholy take over your heart.

You are highly spiritual, and it is a little too easy to drift away and daydream. Stay grounded and present in the here and now or you won't bring your dreams to fruition. This combination can create a restlessness that makes you want to move on rather than face practicalities. Learn to ground yourself in the world by taking consistent action. You are a romantic and you should allow yourself to indulge in fantasies. Just make sure your partners are also on board. Make sure you talk things through with people you care about. Saying something in your head doesn't count. Getting good sleep is essential for your health. If you are not sleeping well, explore options to improve the quality of your sleep.

Pisces rising with your Aquarius Sun opens the gates of the imagination, the dreamworld, and the upperworld. You have a distinctive gift for helping others find their way to other levels of reality. You can tap into other people's emotions as a power source. You can do astral travel, hedge riding, and soul travel in all their forms with some training and practice. You have a gift for interpreting and understanding old magick and updating it so it can be used now. Music, poetry, chanting, and dance also provide fuel for your witchcraft.

A DISH FIT FOR AN AQUARIUS: VISIONARY VIOLET POTATO SOUP

Dawn Aurora Hunt

* * *

Get ready to be intrigued, Aquarian! This dish is deceptively simple and incredibly eccentric. Using purple potatoes, purple cauliflower, and a dash of parmesan, this soup has a distinctive and unexpected look but keeps you grounded in familiar flavors with universal charm. This soup is hearty and comforting but bears the color of pure purple amethyst, tapping into your third eye and bringing intuition and foresight for things to come. Simmering soups are especially magickal and can provide much-needed time for energetic workings. In the case of this dish, use the time it's simmering to visualize a future or goal you are working toward. Lighting a purple candle or having amethyst nearby while making this soup will help enhance the magickal and energetic properties of these ingredients.

Note: This recipe is inherently gluten-free; however, if your diet prohibits you from eating dairy, simply skip the parmesan cheese or replace it with a dairy-free substitute.

Ingredients:

- 1 head purple cauliflower florets
- 3 tablespoons olive oil, divided
- 1 large onion, chopped
- 3 cloves garlic, minced
- 1 pound purple potatoes, peeled and cut into chunks
- 4 cups broth (chicken or vegetable)
- Salt and pepper
- ½ cup grated parmesan cheese
- 1 teaspoon dried oregano
- Fresh sage leaves for topping
- Crème fraîche for topping (optional)

Directions:

Preheat oven to 400 degrees Fahrenheit. In a large bowl, toss cauliflower with two tablespoons olive oil. Roast in the oven about twenty to thirty minutes until tender and slightly brown at the edges. Meanwhile, in a large soup pot or Dutch oven, heat remaining olive oil. Sautee onions and garlic in the oil until tender, do not brown, about five minutes. Add potatoes, broth, salt, and pepper. Simmer until the potatoes are tender, about thirty minutes. By this time, the cauliflower should be cooked. Add the roasted cauliflower to the soup. Using an immersion blender,* puree the soup until silky. Gently stir in the parmesan cheese until it melts in. Top with dried oregano, fresh sage, and crème fraîche if desired.

If you do not have an immersion blender, you can use a regular blender. Blend in small batches and use caution as hot liquids expand in the blender.

RECHARGING AND SELF-CARE

Mickie Mueller

Trying to find balance within the many dual natures that express themselves in an Aquarian witch can leave us feeling overwhelmed or worn out. When that happens, we need to remember to take some time for self-care and recharging our spirit. Recognizing the reasons that an Aquarian can get discombobulated to begin with can be our guide to how we can get back on track and continue our journey as an empowered Aquarian witch.

The life of an Aquarian witch is like a swan on the water—we appear to be aloof as we glide along the water with ease, but beneath that calm surface, our feet are furiously paddling away to keep up the seemingly unflappable and cool exterior. We're a mass of walking contradictions: we look to history, but also innovate; we want to help humanity, but can get exhausted by our fellow humans; we're either highly focused or completely distracted; we love our independence, but yearn to be included.

Aquarians are also perceived as detached, but we feel emotions deeply. We're a water bearer ruled by air. We're that vessel full of emotional waters, and we work very hard to maintain our control over that container, making sure it only pours where it's meant to. When we don't manage our self-care properly, we get tired, and that emotional water jug can spill out where we didn't intend. When that happens, we can only hope that we're somewhere quiet where we can sop up that messy spill without an audience, because that much emotion can embarrass us. Above all, we feel that we must try to maintain our veneer of Mr. Spock—cool and unaffected. After all, anything else would be highly illogical. And that, my dear Aquarius witch cohort, is where self-care comes in.

Balance Thoughts and Emotions

Just like the way Mr. Spock trains his logical Vulcan mind, meditation can be a good place to begin. Even if you're the kind of Aquarian who has a hard time quieting your mind, there are many ways to meditate; if you get bored with one, try another.

Aquarians are a fixed air sign, so no surprise that we tend to get very much in our own heads. We might stuff our feelings down or just numb out. When we do that, our bodies don't process emotions or difficulties. A body-based meditation can be a good way to help us release stagnant emotional energy that we're inevitably holding in our bodies. Somatic body-focused exercises tend to work well for an Aquarian trying to release stress. A guided meditation that includes deep breathing and a body scan where you systematically tense and then relax one part of your body at a time can be very useful. Tapping meditations also known as ETF (Emotional Freedom Technique) have also been shown to help relieve tension in many scholarly peer-reviewed studies, so this form of self-care can appeal to our logical mind. Part of the process of a tapping meditation is that it helps you acknowledge your emotions surrounding a situation while tapping body points to release stress and anxiety. We may prefer to keep some of our emotions out of the public spotlight, which is fine, but looking at them ourselves is very important for healing and ongoing upkeep of our mental and emotional health.

Alternatives to meditation are yoga and tai chi. Both are deeply relaxing. Yoga uses breathing as a way to get in touch with your body, so it's perfect for our fixed air sign. Both yoga and tai chi have many different poses and you can challenge yourself, so you're less likely to get bored with one of these practices.

Forms of meditation and focused movement can help improve our concentration not just in mundane life but in our witchcraft. When you're used to meditating regularly, it's quicker and easier to reach a state of focus that will improve not only your spiritual development but your ability to cast successful spells. Raising, manipulating, and sending energy for spell work will take some training of your mind; this is something meditation can refine. I've also discovered that getting used to how my emotions feel in my body has been of great benefit to my psychic development. It can be hard to tell if you're experiencing intuition or an emotional trigger that's been tripped. When you are used to using these somatic methods to get in touch and better understand your own mind and emotions, it can help you discern the difference between intuition and anxiety. For me, intuition feels more like a calm message coming in; it makes you feel very present and comes from a grounded place. I've found that anxiety feels like it's coming from inside you. It's very worry focused and may activate flight-or-fight response. That's why recognizing these feelings through somatic practices can train your mind and help you tune in to your intuition from a place of calm knowing. This is just one way that self-care can help the Aquarian witch get in touch with our innate abilities.

Let That Beautiful Mind Out to Play

Aquarians are highly creative, so giving yourself some extra time to paint, sculpt, cook, or play an instrument just for recreation can be very healing. Time to sit and read a book or work a puzzle if that's your thing can be very healing too. The idea with all of these is to give your brain a bit of space just to play a bit, and because we Aquarians can get bored easily, keep a list of several choices of brain-friendly fun to help you unwind. We can easily get wrapped up in trying to make a difference in the world around us to the point of exhaustion. We love to feed our heads, so we must allow ourselves opportunities to give that cranium a workout just for fun without it feeling like it needs to be productive or of service to humanity. Sometimes it's healthy to use our brains just for the sake of enjoyment without putting any expectations on the outcome.

Exercising my mind just for fun has helped me release tendencies toward perfectionism, which I tend to express in many of my more serious projects. Giving myself some grace to just exist in my own creativity has helped me when figuring out new innovations in my witchcraft practice without second-guessing myself. Play is vital to creativity, and an important part of witchcraft is creatively imagining your outcome. Allowing your mind judgment-free imagination can grant you the confidence to release attachment surrounding the outcome of a spell, therefore allowing it more space to manifest.

A Tea Practice for the Aquarian Soul

I discovered linden tea a few years ago, and then I learned from Ivo when we were working on this book that linden is an herb that's in alignment with Aquarius energy, and that made so much sense as to why I was drawn to it. Linden has been used throughout history to calm the nervous system, from headaches to digestion and all of your body in between. Those of us who work so hard to keep our very emotional side under wraps can use a witchy brew to release stress and anxiety. Linden is a tree of justice and freedom with beautiful heart-shaped leaves; the tea is made from its flowers. Linden can bring us into the present instead of focusing on regrets of the past or worries about the future. I live in a very small town without a lot of shopping options, so I can't get it locally, but I found Linden tea for the first time at a bodega in St. Louis, and from the first sip, I was convinced that I needed to keep it in my life. I now usually order it online and try to keep it in the house all the time.

You can do this simple enchantment anytime, but it's especially nice to quiet the mind when reading a book or creating something that isn't part of a job but just for you. Brew a cup and add a sweetener of your choice—usually a bit of honey. Then awaken the energy of the tea with this simple incantation whispered over the steaming mug:

Linden tree, come to me,
Soothe my mind, let me just be.

I trace the Aquarius glyph in the air over the top of my tea and press it downward with my projective hand, filling my cup with the spirit of Aquarius. I sip the tea as I read or create and let it soothe my soul.

Harmony Between Shared and Personal Moments

One of the challenges we face is finding harmony between our need for personal independence and our yearning to be part of the bigger picture of society. If we're not careful, we can overpromise our time and energy to group events we enjoy and ignore our need for independence. On the other side of that coin, we might become a bit of a hermit, focusing on our personal time to the detriment of much-needed social interactions with others.

It's important for Aquarians to seek out group activities and set aside time for ourselves and loved ones. As an example, being part of a program that cleans a local state park helps everyone and is a nice way to interact with like-minded people. Enjoying quiet time in that same park with a loved one just experiencing nature is also vital to allowing us to just be our unconventional selves and find our own adventure. Both are important to the Aquarian soul.

Helping Others by Helping Yourself

Self-care is really care for others too. If you're like me, this might be one of those life lessons that keeps coming up for you again and again. I've used the classic adage that comes from the wisdom of flight attendants in the modern age of air travel: "Put your own oxygen mask on first before you help others with theirs." This is because if the airplane cabin's pressure changes, you could pass out, and then you can't help anyone, so you do yours first. I've taught that one to others, you might have too, but are you doing that yourself? I admit I have struggled with it.

We have that aspect of ourselves that leans toward humanitarianism, and if we push that to an extreme, we allow ourselves to come last, but dear Aquarian, you know as well as I do, that's not sustainable. Another adage reminds us, "You can't pour from an empty vessel," meaning that if you refuse to fill yourself up with what you need, you can't support others. It's interesting that the two most common sayings about caring for yourself first before helping others reference air and water. It's almost as if, fellow Aquarius witch, they were trying to get our attention. After years of acting like these lessons applied to everyone but me, I've finally taken them to heart. Yeah, it's a challenge at first, but I can attest that applying this to my own life has made all the difference. I hope it does for you too.

A Self-Care Practice to Soothe the Aquarian Mind

Robin Fennelly

All self-care is intended to bring into balance the physical, mental, and emotional aspects of the individual. The staples of a restorative practice such as journaling and meditation often have the opposite effect on the Aquarian, these being the fertile spaces used to spark new and visionary inspirations. The challenge is selecting protocols that provide a respite from the Aquarius witch's catalytic and strongly energetic magickal workings.

Aquarians are noted for their mental stamina and ability to move from A to Z of any task in a millisecond, replicating the speed and agility of modern technology. This is both the gift of Uranus, Aquarius's ruling planet, and the detriment when attention is not given to tempering the continual stream of electrified energy that pulses through organically.

Accompanying this predisposition is often a disdain for the physical body other than its use as a vehicle to move quickly through the mental processes of corporeal existence. This continued state of mental stimulation requires the cultivation of a soothing practice that both appeals to a curious mind and calms the intensity of that inquiry. Incorporating the gifts of Saturn (the original ruling planet of Aquarius) and its ability to bring awareness to stability and structure provides a complementary grounding to the electrified energy of Uranus and its direct stimulation of the neurologic system.

Daily activities of self-care should include anything that establishes connection with the physical world and allows an emotional response to arise. Walks in nature, feeling the wind move around you, standing in a shallow pool of running water all disengage the mental and shift focus to the physical and emotional. Movement of any kind, in particular yoga, dancing, stretching, and intentional breathing (something Aquarians often forget to do) are opportunities to sink deeply into the physical form and shed any excess of energy.

Meditation can be effective if it is employed as a more structured form that guides rather than allows for open-ended creativity and focuses on natural settings such as gardens, beaches, a tranquil forest, or a cozy cottage.

A Simple Visualization to Get You Started

Begin by sitting in a quiet setting where you will not be disturbed. Take a few deep breaths, gently close your eyes, and let your awareness rise up to the space of your third eye. As you relax into the next exhalation, you envision yourself sitting in a comfortable chair in front of a lit fireplace. You hear the crackling sounds and smell the wafting aroma of burning wood.

The room is dimly lit and you feel the quiet calm that comes at the end of a satisfying day. The last hues of a sunset can be seen from a curtained window and the night settles in, calling you to rest. All your senses are engaged in this setting of absolute stillness. Let yourself rest in this space for as long as you need, and with each passing moment, the stillness flows to restore your body and soothe your mind. When you feel restored, allow the room and fireplace to fade. Breathe deeply into your body and gently flutter your eyes open. Hold the memory of this calm state of mind as you weave your Aquarian magick!

DON'T BLAME IT ON YOUR SUN SIGN

Mickie Mueller

Aquarian traits express themselves differently in each of us. Aquarians are different from non-Aquarians, but we're also each unique among our Sun sign siblings. We have some excellent strengths, but we have our challenges as well. These aren't excuses for the way we show up in life, but traits that we can decide to reinforce or subdue according to our will. Recognizing which traits cause limiting beliefs in ourselves or disharmony with people we care about is really a powerful first step because one area where Aquarian witches shine is in our problem-solving abilities.

Become Friends with Time Spell

If you find that you're often late getting places or you feel like you're not sure where the day went, welcome to the club! In addition to being an Aquarian who struggles with time (because we are ruled by contrasting planetary forces: Uranus, which shatters or fetters time, and Saturn, which places linear restrictions on time), I'm also neurodivergent, which gives me a double whammy where time is involved. The good news for my Aquarian witch friends is that I've done tons of research on time blindness, and although I haven't completely solved it, I've got a spell that includes a work-around that has helped me and might just help you too.

You will need:

- ✦ A timer (not a phone)
- ✦ A picture or symbol of Uranus
- ✦ A blue or white candle for Uranus
- ✦ A picture or symbol of Saturn
- ✦ A black or white candle for Saturn

Instructions:

Place the picture and candle of Uranus on the left side of your workspace and the picture and candle of

Saturn on the right; place your timer between them.
Light the Uranus candle first and say,

> *Uranus, planet that fetters and shatters time,*
> *pushing limits, unpredictable innovator.*

Next, light the Saturn candle and say,

> *Saturn, planet of linear time, hyperfocused,*
> *steward of boundaries.*

Now touch your timer and say,

> *With this tool I seek balance between these*
> *two planetary forces.*
> *When unbound by time it unleashes my mind,*
> *When minding the clock, I manifest goals,*
> *I charge this tool as my guardian of time,*
> *To aid my agenda, fulfilling both roles.*

Trace the Aquarius sigil on the timer with your
finger, or if you want to add it with paint, marker, or
a sticker, you can do that too. Let the candles burn
down with the timer between them.

Use your timer when you need to get a better
handle on time in your life. The pomodoro technique

179

is named after a tomato-shaped kitchen timer. You'll no doubt have fun researching it, but here are the basics.

You can set your timer and say, "I'll do this thing I'm not into, but I only have to do it for twenty minutes." This tricks your brain into starting a task; you'll probably continue on after the timer goes off. If you're deep into a fun creative project you love, set the timer to go off every twenty to thirty minutes to help you keep in touch with how long you're at it, especially if you need to do anything else that day. You can also use it to gamify boring tasks—which is Aquarian kryptonite—such as seeing how many emails you can get through in ten minutes.

Being a Self-Aware Aquarian

The world is a fascinating place full of exciting things to see and do and it's easy to follow our nose from one shiny new thing to the next. At the heart of an Aquarian, however, lives a person who really wants to make a difference in the world, and that difference must start with ourselves. As much as we enjoy analyzing things, figuring out what makes ourselves tick can be fascinating and helps us understand the world around us. If we take time to be more self-aware, it can help us improve our interpersonal skills. We might not want to let others in on how we're feeling and that's okay. Keeping a journal to track moods and emotions can help us identify triggers while helping us release those emotions in a healthy way, and in a way that feels safe to us.

Connect with Others Spell Jar

In the sci-fi series *Doctor Who*, the Doctor could roam through time and space alone, but chooses to bring companions along because they keep the Doctor grounded, compassionate, and it's just more fun. We Aquarian witches can get so distracted with how interesting life is, we can forget to keep our connections with the people who are important to us. Here's a quick spell and an easy mundane action you can do to be more mindful about keeping up communication in your relationships.

You will need:

- ✦ A small jar
- ✦ Incense of your choice
- ✦ Small slip of paper and pen
- ✦ Any or all these ingredients:
  - – allspice for focusing on communication
  - – dried Malva Zebrina (hollyhock) petals for passionate conversation
  - – dried lemon peel for love and friendship
  - – sugar to sweeten

- yarrow for connecting with people
- rosemary for remembrance
- clear quartz for listening and amplifying communication
- amethyst to elevate conversations
- rose quartz for compassion
- sugilite for emotional exchanges
✦ Yellow ribbon
✦ Yellow sealing wax, candle, or additional ribbon

Instructions:

Use incense smoke to purify the bottle and ingredients. Write down at least five people you wish you were better about keeping in touch with. Roll the list into a scroll small enough to fit in your jar and tie it with yellow ribbon or string. Add it to the jar followed by the rest of the ingredients one by one, focusing on each one's purpose in your spell jar. Whisper into the jar your promise to have more communication with the people on your list. Put the lid on the jar and seal it with sealing or candle wax. Alternately, you can wrap ribbon around the lid to seal. Place the jar where you'll notice it daily.

Add alerts to your phone for each person and decide what day and time you want to be reminded to send a text, phone call, or even visit. Don't overcommit; if it's not realistic, you'll be less likely to follow through. One person might be a weekly text while another might be a weekly phone call and monthly afternoon visit. Consider their schedule and yours and feel free to add a time limit. A short call is better than no call when you're working on forging deeper relationships.

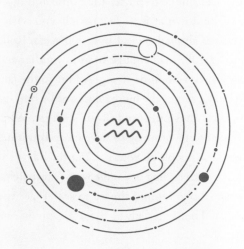

Helping Instead of Ruling

Aquarian witches love to help. We have many ideas on how to solve the world's problems. Nothing's wrong with that on the surface, but we need to be careful that how we're helping is in alignment with the greater good, and not just our personal vision of it. We're free-spirited and open-minded, but we're also a fixed air sign, so yeah, we tend to have strong unwavering opinions. When we're working with a group or helping family members, we should be careful that we're not ruling with an iron fist, but rather summoning our natural compassion, listening to people, and working with them in harmony instead of suffocating them with our pragmatic logic.

I've learned that there is a correlation between increasing the feelings of warmth for others and the warmth for ourselves. This is a practice that seems simple on the surface but can bring powerful shifts. My awesome therapist taught me this one, and I want to share it with you because this inner work increases our compassion for others as well as self-compassion. It's a win for us and everyone we interact with.

Metta or Loving-Kindness Meditation

You might wish to hold a rose quartz, sugilite, or garnet during this meditation or burn Aquarian incense. Find a quiet place to relax; this can be seated or lying down. You know what works best for you. Work with your breath to deepen relaxation and connect with your Aquarius witch energy while closing your eyes. Imagine the Aquarius glyph before you, breathe in healing light along the top wave, breathe out stress along the bottom wave. You can find various versions of Metta or loving-kindness scripts and recorded guided meditations online, but here is essentially how to do it.

Focus on your heart. As you do this, think about a person (or pet) who has always been there for you with unconditional love and support. Imagine they are right there with you and think about how they make you feel. As that loving-kindness they have for you fills your heart, repeat these words or something similar aloud or in your mind.

May I be happy.
May I be at peace.
May I feel safe.
May I be healthy in mind, body, and spirit.

Repeat a few times if you wish until you really feel it.

Next, bring someone to mind whom you love deeply and whom you help with your kindness regularly. Think about the good things you wish for them.

Repeat the following:

May you be happy.
May you be at peace.
May you feel safe.
May you be healthy in mind, body, and spirit.

Next, bring up someone you only know in passing: your favorite barista, the helpful postal worker, or a nice neighbor you interact with occasionally. Use the "may you be happy" script as you think about them, wishing them well.

The next step is optional, but I have found it to be very useful. Imagine someone you don't get along with. This doesn't have to be someone who's harmed you, but someone whom you have some negative feelings about. It can help if you imagine them as a child when they were vulnerable and before you had a problem with them. If you decide you can include them in your well-wishes, use the "may you be happy" script as you think about them, wishing them well. This step helps us realize if these wishes become true for any person, they can improve how they interact with the world.

You can follow this up by repeating the script while imagining all the beings living on Earth, which may include people, animals, and plants. As you end the practice, wiggle your fingers and toes and open your eyes, coming back to regular consciousness.

You're Doing Just Fine

Finding work-arounds for traits that might block our shine under certain circumstances can help us grow in new and exciting ways and make life easier for us and the people in our lives. Most personality features are neither positive nor negative but can be helpful depending on the course of events. When we decide not to blame the expressions of our personalities on our sign and instead find ways to take control of our own inner world, we can embrace our authentic selves and reach the full potential of our Aquarian power.

Aquarius Witch: Altar for the Rebel Mystic

Sandra Santiago

You are here to heed the call of transformation and work against the status quo. Here are some ways that being an Aquarius might shape your practice as a witch:

As an Aquarius, you are often willing to try new things and experiment with different approaches. This may mean that you are more likely to explore fewer mainstream forms of witchcraft, such as chaos magick or pop culture witchcraft.

You may prioritize social justice in your spiritual practice. You are likely to be concerned with social issues. This means that you focus your skills as a practitioner of magick to create positive changes in the world by working for the greater good and protection of marginalized communities.

You may be interested in practicing with a group of like-minded individuals, such as a coven or other spiritual groups. Although, you won't think twice about heeding the call to be a solo practitioner of whatever pantheon you are drawn to work with.

Ideas for Creating an Aquarius Altar

Your altar is a form of creative expression where you can place *anything* special and meaningful to you to focus your practices. As you begin to set up an altar, focus on the color blue as you embellish your altar with pieces that will connect your energy with Uranus.

You may wish to create sigils, symbols to represent a particular intention. You can create a sigil that represents the energy of Uranus connected with the Aquarius glyph of two stacked waves flowing on top of each other.

You can place a combination of crystals specific to Aquarius and Uranus on your altar. Here are five crystals I recommend:

- Garnet is a powerful energizing and regenerating stone. It revitalizes, purifies, and balances energy, bringing serenity or passion as is appropriate at the time.
- Amethyst is associated with the crown chakra and is known to bridge the gap between the physical and spiritual realms. Good for spiritual healing, calmness, and wisdom.
- Aquamarine helps you sift through energy and information, create mental clarity, and soothe an overactive mind.
- Crystal quartz enhances spiritual growth, spirituality, and wisdom because it clarifies thought processes and emotions.
- Aventurine is connected to the heart chakra and supports grounding and stability. For the over-thinking Aquarian who gets stuck in the loop between head and heart, green aventurine will help bring you back into balance.

Now that you've set up your altar, it's time to use your magickal gifts to focus on the energy of Uranus and begin your work. Anoint a blue candle with Uranus oil (equal parts musk, sandalwood, and rose) and light it up. Use this time to attract the qualities of the planet or to worship or invoke the god Uranus. Visualize the planet and its energy flowing through you, bringing inspiration and innovation to your life. You are on your way to the manifestation of your intentions! However, as you do your work, remember to embrace change. One of the most significant qualities associated with Uranus is change.

POSTCARD FROM AN AQUARIUS WITCH
Witching to the Beat of My Own Drum
Kieran

The first thing that came to mind when asked to write for this book is that being an Aquarius shows up in my magickal practice and life as a rather extreme inclination toward independence and self-determinism. As a child, in my pre-witch days, my interests tended toward topics that were questioned by and usually not shared with other family members. But, being an Aquarian, no one was ever successful in dissuading me from pursuing any-thing I truly wanted to pursue. And now, as a witch nearing my mid-thirties, my conviction to follow my chosen path is as strong as ever.

I think this Aquarian influence led me to question my Chris-tian upbringing and start looking into witchcraft and the occult in the first place. My initial gateway into witchcraft was divina-tion. A college friend of mine was interested in learning tarot and asked me if I wanted to learn with him. His interests were purely psychological. For me, it was an excuse to buy my first deck. This was my first tangible step along a winding and sometimes confusing path in which I am both the walker and the creator. Shortly after that first step, I gained the courage to seek out formal training.

For years I looked into several teachers and traditions of witchcraft, even gaining initiation into one. I did distance cor-respondence training, read books, and learned from other witches directly at festivals. With each new group, I was exposed to things that resonated and some that didn't. I became frustrated every time I started working with a new tradition and later realized it wasn't a fit. However, there were many themes I began to pick up on and elements I adopted into my personal practice. During one of these periods of frustration, I consciously chose to stop searching and look around. I took a second to stop walking along the path, look around, and regain my bearings. I looked back on the journey and realized that it was okay I didn't resonate with any of the traditions I joined in the past. I had to ask myself the question that I imagine a lot of other Aquarians have asked themselves: "Why should I follow someone else's path when I could forge my own?"

Using the foundational practices and knowledge I had picked up from teachers over the years as a base, I dove heavily into the three elements that resonated with me the most over the years (folk magick, bioregional witchcraft, and ancestor veneration) to build a craft and set of practices of my very own. I've come far along this path of my own design and still have a long way to go. But, so far, every step has been more fulfilling than the last. Ironically, another Aquarian influence that shows up alongside this deep need for independence in my craft is an equally deep need for there to be other people for me to share and build community with while I walk this path. It is there where I think I have the most room to grow.

• SPIRIT OF AQUARIUS GUIDANCE RITUAL •

Ivo Dominguez, Jr.

The signs are more than useful constructs in astrology or categories for describing temperaments; they are also powerful and complicated spiritual entities. So, what is meant when we say a sign is a spirit? I often describe the signs of the zodiac as the twelve forms of human wisdom and folly. The signs are twelve styles of human consciousness, which also means the signs are well-developed group minds and egregores. Think on the myriad of people over thousands of years who have poured energy into the constructs of the signs through intentional visualization and study. Moreover, the lived experience of each person as one of the signs is deposited into the group minds and egregores of their sign. Every Aquarius who has ever lived or is living contributes to the spirit of Aquarius.

The signs have a composite nature that allows them to exist in many forms on multiple planes of reality at once. In addition to the human contribution to their existence, the spirits of the signs are made from inputs from all living beings in our world, whether they are made of dense matter or of spiritual substances. These vast and ancient thoughtforms that became group minds and then egregores are also vessels that can be used by divine beings to communicate with humans. The spirits of the signs can manifest themselves as small as a sprite or larger than the Earth. The shape and the magnitude of the spirit of Aquarius emerging before you will depend on who you are and how and why you call upon them.

There are many good ways to be a witch and a multitude of well-developed approaches to performing rituals. The ritual described in this chapter may or may not match your accustomed style, but for your first attempt, I encourage you to try it as it is written. Once you've experienced it, then you'll see which parts, if any, you wish to adjust to be a better fit for you. I'll give some suggestions on how to do so at the end of this chapter.

Purpose and Use

This ritual will make it possible to commune with the spirit of Aquarius. The form the spirit will take will be different each time you perform the ritual. What appears will be determined by what you are looking for and your state of mind and soul. The process for preparing yourself for the ritual will do you good as well. Aligning yourself with the source and core of your energy is a useful practice in and of itself. Exploring your circumstances, motivations, and intentions is a valuable experience whether or not you are performing this ritual.

If you have a practical problem you are trying to solve or an obstacle that must be overcome, the spirit of Aquarius may have useful advice. If you are trying to better understand who you are and what you are striving to accomplish, then the spirit of Aquarius can be your mentor. Should you have a need to recharge yourself or flush out stale energy, you can use this ritual to reconnect with a strong clear current of power that is compatible with your core. This energy can be used for magickal empowerment, physical vitality, or healing, or redirected for spell work. If you are charging objects or magickal implements with Aquarius energy, this ritual can be used for this purpose as well.

Timing for the Ritual

The prevailing astrological conditions have an impact on how you experience a ritual, the type and amount of power available, and the outcomes of the work. If you decide you want to go deeper in your studies of astrology, you'll find many simple or elaborate techniques to either pick the best day and time or to adjust your ritual to work with what fits your schedule. Thankfully, the ritual to meet the spirit of your sign does not require exact timing or perfect astrological conditions. This ritual depends on your inner connection to your Sun sign, so it is not as reliant on the external celestial conditions as some other rituals. Each of us has worlds within ourselves, which include inner landscapes and inner skies. Your birth chart, and the sky that it depicts, burns brightest within you. Although not required, you can improve the effectiveness of this ritual if you use any of the following simple guidelines for favorable times:

+ When the Moon, the Sun, Uranus, or Saturn is in Aquarius.
+ When Uranus trines or sextiles a planet in Aquarius.

- When Saturn trines or sextiles a planet in Aquarius.
- On Saturday, the day of Saturn, and even better at dawn.
- During a thunderstorm.

Materials and Setup

The following is a description of the physical objects that will make it easier to perform this ritual. Don't worry if you don't have all of them as, in a pinch, you need no props. However, the physical objects will help anchor the energy and your mental focus.

You will need:
- A printout of your birth chart
- A table to serve as an altar
- A chair if you want to sit during the ritual
- A stick or cone of incense and a holder to represent the element of air (if you can't use incense, a cotton ball drizzled with a fragrance will work)
- An assortment of items for the altar that correspond to Aquarius or Uranus (for example, an amethyst, star anise or citrus

peels, and freesia or Malva Zebrina
flowers)
+ A pad and a pen or chalk and a small
blackboard

Before beginning the ritual, you may wish to copy the
ritual invocations onto paper or bookmark this chapter and bring the book into the ritual. I find that the
process of writing out the invocation, whether hand-
written or typed, helps forge a better connection with
the words and their meaning. If possible, put the altar
table in the center of your space, and if not, then as
close to due east as you can manage. Place the incense
on the altar and hold your hand over it. Send electric
blue sparks of energy from your hand to the incense.
Put the printout of your birth chart on the altar to
one side of the petals and arrange the items you have
selected to anchor the Aquarius and Uranus energy
around them. To the other side of the incense, place
the pad and pen. Make sure you turn off your phone,
close the door, close the curtains, or do whatever
else is needed to prevent distractions. Now light the
incense before proceeding. Take a moment to catch its
scent and hold it in your memory.

Ritual to Meet the Spirit of Your Sign

You may stand or be seated; whichever is the most comfortable for you. Begin by focusing on your breathing. When you pay attention to the process of breathing, you become more aware of your body, the flow of your life energy, and the balance between conscious and unconscious actions. After you have done so for about a minute, it is time to shift into fourfold breathing. This consists of four phases: inhaling, lungs full, exhaling, and lungs empty. You count to keep time so that each of the four phases is of equal duration. Try a count of four or five in your first efforts. Depending on your lungs and how fast you count, you will need to adjust the number higher or lower. When you hold your breath, hold it with your belly muscles, not your throat. When you hold your breath in fourfold breathing, your throat should feel relaxed. Be gentle and careful with yourself if you have asthma, high blood pressure, are late in pregnancy, or have any other condition that may have an impact on your breathing and blood pressure. In general, if there are difficulties, they arise during the lungs' full or empty phases because of holding them by clenching the throat or compressing the lungs. The empty and the full lungs should be held by the position of the diaphragm, and the air passages left open. After one to three minutes of fourfold breathing, you can return to your normal breathing pattern.

Now, close your eyes and move your center of consciousness down into the middle of your chest. Proceed with grounding and centering, dropping and opening, shifting into the alpha state, or whatever practice you use to reach the state of mind that supports ritual work. Then gaze deeply inside yourself and find yourself sitting on the ground in a garden. Look at the beauty of the crystal and the plant materials. Take a breath and smell fresh air and refreshing fragrances. Pick up the incense holder and gently move the air with it and awaken all the places and spaces within you that are of Aquarius. When you feel ready, open your eyes.

Zodiac Casting

If you are seated, stand if you are able and face the east. Slowly read this invocation aloud, putting some energy into your words. As you read, slowly turn counterclockwise so that you come full circle when you reach the last line. Another option is to hold your hand over your head and trace the counterclockwise circle of the zodiac with your finger.

I call forth the twelve to join me in this rite.
I call forth Aries and the power of courage.
I call forth Taurus and the power of stability.
I call forth Gemini and the power of versatility.
I call forth Cancer and the power of protection.
I call forth Leo and the power of the will.
I call forth Virgo and the power of discernment.
I call forth Libra and the power of harmony.
I call forth Scorpio and the power of renewal.
I call forth Sagittarius and the power of vision.
I call forth Capricorn and the power of
*   responsibility.*
I call forth Aquarius and the power of
*   innovation.*
I call forth Pisces and the power of compassion.
The power of the twelve is here.
Blessed be!

Take a few deep breaths and shift your gaze to each of the items on the altar. Become aware of the changes in the atmosphere around you and the presence of the twelve signs.

Altar Work

Pick up the printout of your birth chart and look at your chart. Touch each of the twelve houses with your finger and push energy into them. You are energizing and awakening your birth chart to act as a focal point of power on the altar. Put your chart back on the altar when it feels ready to you. Then take the pad and pen and write the glyph for Aquarius again and again. The glyphs can be different sizes, they can overlap; you can make any pattern with them you like so long as you pour energy into the ink as you write. Scribing the glyph is an action that helps draw the interest of the spirit of Aquarius. Periodically look at the items on the altar as you continue scribing the glyph. When you feel sensations in your body, such as electric tingles, warmth, shivers, or something that you associate with the approach of a spirit, it is time to move on to the next step. If these are new experiences for you, just follow your instincts. Put away the pen and paper and pick up the sheet with the invocation of Aquarius.

Invoking Aquarius

Before beginning to read this invocation, get in touch with your feelings. Think on what you hope to accomplish in this ritual and why it matters to you. Then speak these lines slowly and with conviction.

> *Aquarius, hear me, for I am born of the*
> *wind's fixed air.*
> *Aquarius, see me, for the Aquarius Sun*
> *shines upon me.*
> *Aquarius, know me as a member of your*
> *family and your company.*
> *Aquarius, know me as your student and your*
> *protégé.*
> *Aquarius, know me as a conduit for your*
> *power.*
> *Aquarius, know me as a wielder of your*
> *magick.*
> *I am of you, and you are of me.*
> *I am of you, and you are of me.*
> *I am of you, and you are of me.*
> *Aquarius is here within and without.*
> *Blessed be!*

Your Requests

Close your eyes and look within for several deep breaths, and silently or aloud welcome the spirit of Aquarius. Close your eyes and ask for any guidance that would be beneficial for you and listen. It may take some time before anything comes through, so be patient. I find it valuable to receive guidance before making a request so that I can refine or modify intentions and outcomes. Consider the meaning of whatever impressions or guidance you received and reaffirm your intentions and desired outcomes for this ritual.

It is more effective to use multiple modes of communication to make your request. Speak silently or aloud the words that describe your need and how it could be solved. Visualize the same message but without the words and project the images on your mind's screen. Then put all your attention on your feelings and your bodily sensations that have been stirred up by contemplating your appeal to the spirit of Aquarius. Once again wait and use all your physical and psychic senses to perceive what is given. At this point in the ritual, if there are objects to be charged, touch them or focus your gaze on them.

Offer Gratitude

You may be certain or uncertain about the success of the ritual or the time frame for the outcomes to become clear. Regardless of that, it is a good practice to offer thanks and gratitude to the spirit of Aquarius for being present. Also, thank yourself for doing your part of the work. The state of heart and mind that comes with thanks and gratitude makes it easier for the work to become manifest. Thanks and gratitude also act as a buffer against the unintended consequences that can be put into motion by rituals.

Release the Ritual

If you are seated, stand if you are able and face the east. Slowly turn clockwise until you come full circle while repeating the following or something similar.

> *Return, return oh turning wheel to your starry home.*
> *Farewell, farewell brilliant Aquarius until we speak again.*

Another option while saying these words is to hold your hand over your head and trace a clockwise circle of the zodiac with your finger. When you are done, look at your chart on the altar and say,

It is done. It is done. It is done.

Afterward

I encourage you to write down your thoughts and observations of what you experienced in the ritual. Do this while it is still fresh in mind before the details begin to blur. The information will become more useful over time as you work more with the spirit of Aquarius. It will also let you evaluate the outcomes of your workings and improve your process in future workings. This note-taking or journaling will also help you dial in any changes or refinements to this ritual for future use. Contingent upon the guidance you received or the outcomes you desire, you may want to add reminders to your calendar.

More Options

These are some modifications to this ritual you may wish to try:

+ Put together or purchase Aquarius incense to burn during the ritual. An

Aquarius oil to anoint the crystal or yourself is another possibility.

+ Set up a richer and deeper altar. In addition to adding more objects that resonate to the energy of Aquarius or Uranus, consecrate each object before the ritual. You may also want to place an altar cloth on the table that brings to mind Aquarius, Uranus, or the element of air.

+ Creating a sigil to concentrate the essence of what you are working toward would be a good addition to the altar.

+ Consider adding chanting, free-form toning, or movement to raise energy for the altar work and/or for invoking Aquarius.

+ If you feel inspired, you can write your own invocations for calling the zodiac and/or invoking Aquarius. This is a great way to deepen your understanding of the signs and to personalize your ritual.

Rituals have greater personal meaning and effectiveness when you personalize them and make them your own.

AQUARIUS ANOINTING OIL RECIPE

* * *

Ivo Dominguez, Jr.

This oil is used for charging and consecrating candles, crystals, and other objects you use in your practice. This oil makes it easier for an object to be imbued with Aquarius energy. It also primes and tunes the objects so your will and power as an Aquarius witch flow more easily into them. Do not apply the oil to your skin unless you have done an allergy test first.

Ingredients:
+ Carrier oil—1 ounce
+ Lavender—6 drops
+ Benzoin—5 drops
+ Basil—4 drops
+ Cypress—4 drops
+ Star anise—2 drops

Pour one ounce of a carrier oil into a small bottle or vial. The preferred carrier oils are almond oil or fractionated coconut oil. Other carrier oils can be used. If you use olive oil, the blend will have a shorter shelf life. Ideally use essential oils, but fragrance oils can be used as substitutes. Add the drops of the essential oils into the carrier. Once they are all added, cap the bottle tightly, and shake the bottle several times. Hold the bottle in your hands, take a breath, and pour energy into the oil. Visualize electric blue energy or repeat the word *Aquarius* or raise energy in your preferred manner. Continue doing so until the oil feels warm, seems to glow, or you sense it is charged.

Label the bottle and store the oil in a cool, dark place. Consider keeping a little bit of each previous batch of oil to add to the new batch. This helps build the strength and continuity of the energy and intentions you have placed in the oil. Over time, that link makes your oils more powerful.

• BETTER EVERY DAY: THE WAY FORWARD •

Mickie Mueller

now that we have dug into what being an Aquarian witch means to us, let's think about ways to bring that specific aspect of ourselves to the forefront of our daily magickal practice. I love exploring ways to become a better magickal practitioner, finding more effective methods for my spells and spiritual practices and feeding my spiritual growth. Even small changes can create big benefits.

Embracing Your Aquarius Authenticity All Day Long

Part of being an Aquarian witch is embracing that decision to live in the moment and change things to suit your mood and hold your interest. No matter your state of mind from one day to the next, there are mini practices you can add throughout the day to always shift yourself back toward your authentic Aquarian power.

Get Outside

Even if you only have a few minutes out of a busy day, you'll activate your Aquarian witch power by spending a bit of time in nature. That might mean a long walk in the woods or five minutes looking at the spaces between branches of a tree growing near your home. A quick nature break can bring you back to your power.

Bite-Sized Mental Stimulation

Instead of mind-dulling doomscrolling while you're waiting in line or on a coffee break, curate some apps that engage your intellect. Try a library app where you can grab your next witchy read. Mix it up with a puzzle game you really like, an app that teaches you tarot, a creative coloring app, a stargazing app that shows where all the constellations are at any given moment like a mobile planetarium. Group them on your phone in a folder and call it "Aquarius" so they're easier to find than your social media apps.

Have a Touchstone

Choose a piece of magickal jewelry or pocket piece that you can come back to in meaningful moments during your day. An amethyst or garnet either set in a ring, necklace, or a funky bracelet can give you something to help you connect mindfully to your purpose of being true to your power. Equally, you can use symbols of Aquarius like a charm of your glyph, constellation, or water bearer on jewelry, in your pocket, or even in a tattoo. Just touching these items before a big meeting, during lunch with a friend, or while you're looking for inspiration for your next big idea can spark that Aquarian energy to life.

Habit Stacking

Aquarians get bored easily, and positive reinforcement helps keep us engaged. If you stack a habit you are trying to implement like doing a daily tarot card pull, try including it as part of your morning coffee routine as you contemplate your card over your favorite brew. Pair getting that twenty-minute nature walk in with something you already enjoy, like listening to your favorite witchcraft podcast, and you'll be more likely to do that walk. What are other habits you can stack?

Affirmations in the Stream of Aquarius Energy

You can use the following eleven affirmations in any way you like to help activate your most beneficial Aquarian traits and inspire creative work-arounds for your challenges in true Aquarian style. Why eleven? We're the eleventh sign in the zodiac, of course! You can repeat them all in one stream or pick one to focus on and internalize one at a time. You might like to use them at the start or end of your day. You can also pick one to use as a focus throughout your day. These would be perfect to incorporate into different spells to help embrace your personal power. I hope you find these useful, and since you're an innovative Aquarian too, maybe they'll inspire you to come up with more.

+ I am connected to my Aquarian witch energy, consciously stepping into my flow of power.

+ I am secure in my own weirdness; it's a feature, not a bug.

+ The obstacles others see are just catalysts for my innovative spirit.

+ I remember my purpose and move through worlds to manifest my goals.

+ It's safe to connect with other people in an open and compassionate way.

+ When I recognize self-judgment, I can release my judgment of others.

+ I honor and support the freedom and individuality of others as well as my own.

+ I am one with everything, but also unique and express my individuality.

+ My creativity is like lightning striking the source of my witch's power.

+ I am living in alignment with my values.

+ I fearlessly blaze trails forward through limitless possibilities.

Evening Self-Care to Rest and Reset

The night is a good time to give ourselves extra support through a simple but powerful evening practice. Since late night is a power time for Aquarius witches, even if we're not staying up late for a big spell or ritual, we can tap into that energy. I'll share my bedtime practice that facilitates my connection with my Aquarian witch power all night.

When I'm ready to unwind, I wash my face, releasing not only cosmetics and physical buildup, but also spiritual residue from any masking or code-switching that I was required by society to perform throughout the day. I reveal my bare face and allow myself to just exist in my own skin, and of course, moisturize. I grab a cup of calming tea. To add an extra layer of Aquarian magick, I like something with orange blossoms, vervain, or linden flower, but if you can't find those ingredients, that's okay, just use what's available. Next, I make sure I have a dream journal and pen on my bedside table or open the notes app on my phone. Even if I'm not staying up late for a spell or ritual, I've found my Aquarian brain may work on problems, inspiration, or divination while my conscious mind rests. The best way to capture those fleeting dreams is to document them quickly before my feet hit the floor.

My favorite part of this evening ritual relates to the part of the body ruled by Aquarius. I remember the first time I saw a vintage diagram showing which parts of the body are ruled by each Sun sign, and there was an arrow piercing through the figure's calves next to the image of the water bearer. Yikes! With my nighttime leg cramps and plantar fasciitis, I could absolutely relate to that. Yes, we Aquarians can lean toward circulation, muscle, and even skin problems in this part of our body. Some aromatherapy care in this area can be a beautiful way to get that active mind to unwind at the end of the day while harnessing the power of air to connect to your Aquarian spirit.

Ivo suggests neroli as a flower that's good for protection for Aquarians, so I ordered some neroli lotion to keep next to my bed. I wanted a little stronger scent, so I added three extra drops of neroli oil to the bottle and shook it up. I used a permanent marker to inscribe the Aquarian glyph onto the bottom of the lotion bottle and then charged it. I charged it on a Saturday, but you can also check your astrological calendar for auspicious Aquarian timing. I love to use it to rub into my skin from my calves down to my feet before I go to sleep, giving extra care to the part of my body that's ruled by Aquarius. Magickally, neroli is protective; its fresh, slightly citrusy spring floral scent also promotes relaxation by soothing your nervous system and promoting sleep and even lucid dreaming. Since I started adding this practice to my nighttime ritual, my sleep has been more rejuvenating, and my dreams have been more vivid. I've even had some problem-solving dreams. As always, use care with essential oils; don't use full strength and add a few drops to a carrier oil instead. Check with a doctor before using any essential oil if you're pregnant or nursing or have any other health concerns.

Embrace a Cause You Care About

One of the most beautiful and empowering ways that I have found to really be part of the stream of Aquarius energy is to get in touch with a cause that you care deeply about and support it in both magickal and mundane ways. If we try to fix everything, Aquarian logic reminds us that it's just not plausible. If you could put focused energy into just one cause that you care about deeply, you could make a difference. If all Aquarian witches each picked just one mission to focus on, what could we really accomplish? Yes, you can still have side quests, but with one main goal you can see your effects more clearly, and these little wins can give you more energy to manage a side quest or two as the mood or necessity strikes.

I love performing spells surrounding a great cause. Activism is deeply tied to witchcraft because just being a witch can be considered a rebellious act. Witchcraft wasn't born from living in ease but has often been a tool of the oppressed. When working spells to help a cause you care about, if you're able to include elements that help you tap into your Aquarian energy like stones, herbs, or timing found within this book, it's a good way to boost the efficacy of any spell. Passion for a humanitarian or planetary cause is deep in the flow of Aquarius energy, so it can really move a spell along. Combining magick and mundane action can get the best results. If you're collecting signatures on a petition, charge the pen you use during a spell to attract like-minded people. If you're making phone calls, wear your Aquarius witch jewelry and light some incense for your air element to boost your eloquence. If you're heading to a public event, you could call upon divine guidance for strength and protection for all attending by leaving a sigil drawn on a map of the location on your altar. Finding both spiritual and practical ways to help your cause can be very rewarding and help you feel a strong connection to your community and your own Aquarius witch nature.

CONCLUSION

Ivo Dominguez, Jr.

no doubt, you are putting what you discovered in this book to use in your witchcraft. You may have a desire to learn more about how astrology and witchcraft fit together. One of the best ways to do this is to talk about it with other practitioners. Look for online discussions, and if there is a local metaphysical shop, check to see if they have classes or discussion groups. If you don't find what you need, consider creating a study group. Learning more about your own birth chart is also an excellent next step.

At some point, you may wish to call upon the services of an astrologer to give you a reading that is fine-tuned to your chart. There are services that provide not just charts but full chart readings that are generated by software. These are a decent tool and more economical than a professional astrologer, but they lack the finesse and intuition that only a person can offer. Nonetheless, they can be a good starting point. If you do decide to hire an astrologer to do your chart, shop around to find someone attuned to your spiritual needs. You may decide to learn enough astrology to read your own chart, and that will serve you for many reasons. However, for the same reasons that tarot readers will go to someone else for a reading, the same is true with astrological readers. It is hard to see some things when you are too attached to the outcomes.

If you find your interest in astrology and its effect on a person's relationship to witchcraft has been stimulated by this book, you may wish to read the other books in this series. Additionally, if you have other witches you work with, you'll find that knowing more about how they approach their craft will make your collective efforts more productive. Understanding them better will also help reduce conflicts or misunderstandings. The ending of this book is really the beginning of an adventure. Go for it.

APPENDIX
AQUARIUS CORRESPONDENCES

January 20/21–February 18/20

Symbol: ♒

Solar System: Neptune, Saturn, Uranus

Season: Winter

Day: Saturday

Runes: Hagal, Sigel

Element: Air

Colors: Blue (Dark), Green, Indigo, Silver, Turquoise, Violet, Yellow (Light, Pale)

Energy: Yang

Chakras: Throat, Brow, Crown

Number: 11

Tarot: Swords, Fool, Star

Trees: Acacia, Apple, Ash, Aspen, Cherry, Cypress, Hawthorn, Mimosa, Olive, Pine, Rowan

Herb and Garden: Dandelion, Foxglove, Iris, Lavender, Peppermint, Rosemary, Sage, Violet

Miscellaneous Plants: Anise, Bittersweet, Frankincense, Henbane, Myrrh, Patchouli, Sandalwood

Gemstones and Minerals: Agate (Red), Amber, Amethyst, Angelite, Aquamarine, Aventurine, Fluorite, Garnet, Hematite, Jade, Moss Agate, Onyx, Opal, Quartz (Clear), Sapphire, Turquoise, Zircon (Red)

Metals: Aluminum, Lead, Silver

From the Sea: Coral (White), Pearl

Goddesses: Astarte, Ishtar, Isis, Juno, Nut

Gods: Ea

Angels: Gabriel, Raphael

Animals: Dog, Otter, Sheep

Birds: Albatross, Cuckoo, Eagle, Peacock

Mythical: Phoenix

Issues, Intentions, and Powers: Ambition, Charity, Community (Spiritual), Compassion, Cooperation, Creativity, Desire, Determination, Freedom,

Friendship, Gentleness, Healing, Honesty, Hope, Independence, Integrity, Intelligence, Intuition, Light, Loyalty, Peace, Sensitivity, Spirituality, Sympathy, Wisdom

RESOURCES

Online

Astrodienst: Free birth charts and many resources.

+ https://www.astro.com/horoscope

Astrolabe: Free birth chart and software resources.

+ https://alabe.com

The Astrology Podcast: A weekly podcast hosted by professional astrologer Chris Brennan.

+ https://theastrologypodcast.com

Magazine

The world's most recognized astrology magazine (available in print and digital formats).

+ https://mountainastrologer.com

Books

+ *Practical Astrology for Witches and Pagans* by Ivo Dominguez, Jr.
+ *Parkers' Astrology: The Definitive Guide to Using Astrology in Every Aspect of Your Life by* Julia and Derek Parker

- *The Inner Sky: How to Make Wiser Choices for a More Fulfilling Life* by Steven Forrest
- *Predictive Astrology: Tools to Forecast Your Life and Create Your Brightest Future* by Bernadette Brady
- *Chart Interpretation Handbook: Guidelines for Understanding the Essentials of the Birth Chart* by Stephen Arroyo

CONTRIBUTORS

We give thanks and appreciation to all our guest authors who contributed their own special Aquarian energy to this project.

Silver Daniels

Silver Daniels is a Gardnerian HP and Lukumi aborisha, practicing witchcraft for over twenty years. Specializing in occult herbalism and trafficking with spirits, Silver is a familiar face in the magickal community. His Sun, Moon, and Mercury are all placed in Aquarius, making him a witty and charming individual who loves to laugh—but he is serious and knowledgeable when it comes to magick.

Danielle Dionne

Danielle Dionne is an Aquarius, psychic medium, witch, herbalist, homesteader, and author of *Magickal Mediumship*. Danielle is a High Priestess in the Temple of Witchcraft Tradition, serving as Scorpio Deputy Minister. Danielle stewards Crossroads Farm, a small, spirited homestead focused on ancestral connections, magick and medicinal herbalism, and raising heritage-breed livestock in Southern New Hampshire. Visit Danielle at http://danielledionne.com.

Robin Fennelly

Robin Fennelly is an Elder within The Assembly of the Sacred Wheel Tradition. Her magickal journey spans four decades as a practicing witch and occultist. Her blog, *A Witch's Sacred Journey*, features online courses, rituals, spells, and more for the modern witch. Robin's books and teachings can be found at www.robinfennelly.com.

Dawn Aurora Hunt

Dawn Aurora Hunt, owner of Cucina Aurora Kitchen Witchery, is the author of *A Kitchen Witch's Guide to Love & Romance* and *Kitchen Witchcraft for Beginners*. Though not born under the sign of Aquarius, she combines knowledge of spiritual goals and magickal ingredients to create recipes for all Sun signs in this series. She is a Scorpio. Find her at www.CucinaAurora.com.

Kieran

Kieran walks a crooked path of his own making. His craft is guided by the relationships he's forged with spirits, his ancestors, and the land around him. When not communing with the dead or wandering through the woods, Kieran spends quality time with his husband and cat.

Sandra Kynes

Sandra Kynes (Midcoast Maine) is the author of seventeen books, including *Mixing Essential Oils for Magic*, *Magical Symbols and Alphabets*, *Crystal Magic*, *Plant Magic*, and *Sea Magic*. Excerpted content from her book *Llewellyn's Complete Book of Correspondences* has been used throughout this series, and she is a Scorpio. Find her at http://www.kynes.net.

Alexandra Nic Bhé Chuille

Alexandra Nic Bhé Chuille is a pagan polytheist and a modern hedgewitch who currently lives near Washington, DC. She has been an avid fan of tarot since she first encountered it twenty years ago and has been a professional cartomancer for nearly a decade. You can find her online at https://7serendipities.com/team/.

Sandra Santiago

Sandra Santiago is a radical educator, activist, and poet. Sandra is a Lucumi Priestess of Obatala as well as a Yaya Nganga in Palo Mayombe. She is a certified Reiki Master. Sandra is also a medium in Afro-Caribbean Espiritismo. She is a Reiki Master. Her spiritual work can be defined as decolonization therapy.

Notes

Notes

Notes

To Write to the Author

If you wish to contact the author or would like more information about this book, please write to the author in care of Llewellyn Worldwide Ltd. and we will forward your request. Both the author and the publisher appreciate hearing from you and learning of your enjoyment of this book and how it has helped you. Llewellyn Worldwide Ltd. cannot guarantee that every letter written to the author can be answered, but all will be forwarded. Please write to:

Ivo Dominguez, Jr.
Mickie Mueller
℅ Llewellyn Worldwide
2143 Wooddale Drive
Woodbury, MN 55125-2989

Please enclose a self-addressed stamped envelope for reply, or $1.00 to cover costs. If outside the U.S.A., enclose an international postal reply coupon.

Many of Llewellyn's authors have websites with additional information and resources. For more information, please visit our website at:

www.llewellyn.com